THINK
ACT
BELIEVE
LIKE
JESUS

THINK
ACT
BELIEVE
LIKE
JESUS

BECOMING A NEW PERSON IN CHRIST

RANDY FRAZEE
WITH ROBERT NOLAND

ZONDERVAN®

ZONDERVAN

Think, Act, Be Like Jesus
Copyright © 2014 by Randy Frazee

This title is also available as a Zondervan ebook. Visit www.zondervan.com/ebooks.

This title is also available in a Zondervan audio edition. Visit www.zondervan.fm.

Zondervan, 3900 *Sparks Dr. SE, Grand Rapids, Michigan* 49546

Library of Congress Cataloging-in-Publication Data

Frazee, Randy.
    Think, act, be like Jesus : becoming a new person in Christ / Randy Frazee, with
    Robert Noland.
        pages cm
    Includes bibliographical references.
    ISBN 978-0-310-25017-3 (softcover)
        1. Christian life. 2. Spiritual life—Christianity. 3. Theology, Doctrinal. I. Title.
    BV4501.3.F73557 2015
    248.4—dc23   2014025607

Cover design: *Extra Credit Projects*
Interior design: *Beth Shagene*

Printed in the United States of America

14 15 16 17 18 19 20 21 22 23 /DCI/ 19 18 17 16 15 14 13 12 11 10 9 8 7 6 5 4 3 2 1

To Jennifer, David, Stephen, and Austin —
the four children God gave us to raise up in Christ.
You were the motivation for the content of this book.
We are so very proud of who you are becoming —
more and more like Jesus every day!

Contents

PART 3:

Be Like Jesus
Who Am I Becoming?

PART 4:

Transformation

The Confession of Unbelief

I have amazing memories of my mom. She came from a very poor family in southwestern Pennsylvania and married my father at eighteen years old. When I was three, they moved to Cleveland, Ohio, where my dad secured a job with Caterpillar, assembling forklifts.

Throughout my childhood, my mother loved and sacrificed so much for my three siblings and me. She spent all of her money, time, and energy on us. I recall that she rarely did anything for herself. So, several years ago, when I was at a place in my life where I had some financial margin, I called my mother to tell her I was taking her and my dad on an all-expense-paid trip with our family to the magnificent Niagara Falls on the day after Christmas. I reserved rooms in a turn-of-the-century, opulent hotel on the Canadian side, facing the waterfalls. She was going to be so embarrassed and uncomfortable, believing she didn't belong in a place like this — but I wanted her to have an unforgettable experience.

When I called Mom a few months before the trip date, she told me she wasn't feeling well. Initially, I thought she was just trying to wiggle out of the trip. As the next few months unfolded, though, her illness grew worse, and I really began to worry. I decided to fly to my parents' home a few days earlier than we had been scheduled to arrive there — and only a week before our big vacation.

Three days later, my mother died of advanced pancreatic cancer at the age of sixty-two. The trip was canceled only seventy-two hours before we were to leave. I was finally in a position to do something for my mother, and I missed it forever by three days. Three days! I was devastated in so many ways. Something changed within me — maybe more of an awakening of what had been there all along. My soul was in crisis. I slipped into a place of despair.

The thing I miss most about being with my mom is laying my head between her head and shoulders. It was the safest, sweetest place on earth. The last two days of my mom's life, when no one else was in the room, I crawled into the bed with her and placed my head in that warm spot of intense love. Tears rolled down my face. I thought I would have had more time. I was trying to soak in a lifetime in only a few fleeting hours.

Be Like Jesus—VIRTUES

Looking back, I now realize the amazing sense of God's timing. In this season surrounding my mother's illness and death, three spiritual giants were mentoring me. Each was individually "schooling" me on the very work now coming to fruition fifteen years later in this book and in the *Believe* Bible engagement experience. But before these resources could go out to help others, God had decided to do some work *in me* first. The biblical word is *pruning* — the process in which God wants to work *through* us, but first must work *on* us. A deeper work takes place in the individual for the greater work to go out to the world — much like a gardener prunes the trees to gain the best harvest (see John 15:2).

My three spiritual mentors were J. I. Packer,[1] Dallas Willard,[2] and George Gallup Jr.[3]

Here is what my mentors taught me: The Christian life is not primarily an intellectual pursuit; nor is it simply about doing good or engaging in spiritual activity. The Christian life is about who you are becoming for the sake of others. Since Jesus came from heaven to represent us, he also modeled for us the life we were created to live.

Therefore, *the ultimate objective of life by God's design is for us to be like Jesus.*

God's passion is for the virtues of Jesus to appear in our lives. The Bible calls these virtues "fruit." Fruit is external to a tree. It is seen by all and available to taste by all. When delicious fruit appears on the end of our branches, it gives evidence of the health inside. But, ultimately, the value of fruit is for the benefit of others, who grab hold of the fruit of our lives and taste it. Is it ripe, sweet, and delicious, or is it green and rotten, or possibly even artificial?

Paul called these virtues "the fruit of the Spirit." The grape was likely the first fruit to come to the mind of the early Christian, who might have harkened back to the teaching of Jesus about the vine and the branches.

Recently, I watched *Somm*, a documentary about a group of men trying to attain the level of Master Sommelier — the highest level an expert in wines can achieve. Five wines were placed in front of the aspiring contestants. They would swirl the glass, immerse their noses completely inside, and take a deep breath. Then they would take a sip, swish the wine in their mouths, and spit it out in a bucket. From this exercise, they were able to declare the region, variety, date, body, and tannins of the wine. I found the description of the flavor to be fascinating. The word most often used was *hint*. A candidate would say, for example, "This wine has a hint of cinnamon, a hint of oak, a hint of licorice, a hint of blueberry, and a hint of earth."

This may be what Paul had in mind when he gave us the famous list of the fruit of the Spirit in Galatians 5:22 – 23. The virtues of our lives are contained in a glass, so to speak. The neighbor, the wife, or the friend picks up the glass and swirls it, immerses their nose inside and sniffs, and then takes a sip, swishing it around to then declare, "This wine carries hints of love, joy, peace, patience, kindness, goodness, faithfulness, gentleness, and self-control. I am also picking up hints of hope and humility."

The "hint of hope" was missing from my life. And a human

can't live without hope. This explained my state of depression. Up to this point in my life, I had been living out of a false sense of hope. For me, as for many people, I "hoped" life here would be good and stay consistent — to be translated as no relationship crises, no divorce, no disease, no job loss, money in the bank, and certainly no deaths of anyone I love deeply. While such a "hope" may hold up for a while, eventually it will disappoint and fail us. God wants to give us a true hope, rising above all earthly matters and seeing us through all our troubles. Clearly, I didn't have this kind of fruit at the end of my branches. And the death of my mother exposed my need.

Here's a quite interesting fact I learned through this: You can't grow in the virtue of hope by merely trying to be more hopeful. The same is true of all the other fruit — *By golly, I am going to just be more joyful tomorrow.* While it is certainly essential to have a vision for change and growth, it will not come into our lives by simply willing it to be true.

Think Like Jesus — BELIEFS

To find the solution to *being like Jesus*, I went back to my mentors. I found becoming like Jesus requires we *think like Jesus.* Accomplishing this is far harder than it might seem. All three men said the same thing to me, independent of one another: *It is not enough to believe something as the right answer; you must believe it as a way of life.*

The journey of belief begins in the head, but it must migrate twelve inches south to the heart to make a difference in our lives. Why? Because we live from the heart. We live consistent with the beliefs embraced in our hearts.[4]

"As he thinks in his heart, so is he" (Proverbs 23:7 NKJV).

The writer did not say, "As he thinks in his *mind*," but rather, "As he thinks in his *heart.*" There is a vast difference. Consider the context for this verse:

Do not eat the bread of a miser,
Nor desire his delicacies;
For as he thinks in his heart, so is he.
"Eat and drink!" he says to you,
But his heart is not with you.
The morsel you have eaten, you will vomit up,
And waste your pleasant words
(Proverbs 23:6–8 NKJV, emphasis added).

Suppose you spend the night at the house of a person you do not know well. Before he leaves in the morning for work, he tells you to help yourself to whatever is in the refrigerator. So you do. When he comes home, he gives you the cold shoulder. You ask him if there is anything wrong, but he answers, "No." Later in the week, you hear through the gossip chain of friends that, in fact, he was angry with you because you raided his refrigerator. You respond to your friends, "This can't be. He told me it was okay." After your friends chuckle a bit, one quips, "It doesn't matter what he *says*; everyone knows he's a miser. He can't help himself."

Your host knows the proper thing is to offer up the contents of his fridge. However, when it comes right down to the truth, he really doesn't embrace this notion, for in his heart, he is a miser. He lives consistently with the values and principles of a begrudging host. He just can't help himself. Why? Because the belief resides in his heart.

Jesus reinforced this axiom when he said, "Where your treasure is, there your heart will be also" (Matthew 6:21).

If Jesus were speaking to us today, he might say, "Show me your checkbook or credit card bill, and I will tell you what you truly believe." Your money follows the central beliefs of your heart. You can go to a financial management seminar and understand every principle in your head, but what you believe in your heart is what counts and what ultimately determines your spending, saving, and investment habits.

If you struggle to live your beliefs, then you don't really believe them. You might understand; it might be a requirement to give intellectual assent in the community in which you hang out. But the belief has not yet taken up residence in your heart.

Claude Harmon, winner of the 1948 Masters Tournament, where the take-home prize was $2,500, trained all four of his sons into arguably becoming the best golf instructors in the world. My next-door neighbor plays on the PGA tour, and he switched to Butch Harmon last year. He has already won three tournaments this season, with earnings at right around $4 million, before sponsorships. Claude once told his sons, "A *good* golf instructor can spot the ten things wrong with a golfer's swing; a *great* golf instructor can identify the one causing the other nine."

The same is true in the Christian life. A good spiritual coach might be able to spot the ten things wrong with the way I approach life, and even my absence of hope; a great spiritual coach can spot the one thing causing the other nine.

The one thing is almost always a belief — something I don't understand or have never been taught about the Christian life, which is certainly a systemic issue among believers today. Or there is something I believe in my head to be true or right, yet it doesn't reside in my heart, which then undermines my experience of hope.

The journey of belief begins with the confession of unbelief.

This statement is what my mentors were talking about. You have to help people discover this truth, and then they must confess it to themselves and to a few significant others, if they ever want to truly live the Christian life. I know I certainly had to.

So I then asked myself, "What do I *not* believe? What is the cause of this hopelessness?"

As a result of my work with my mentors, I've come to see there are, and always have been, ten essential driving beliefs of orthodox Christianity. Which of these ten was a primary struggle for me, thus hindering my experience of hope?

Dr. J. I. Packer — my "Butch Harmon," my "Master Sommelier" — had some keen insight. Two primary beliefs drive biblical hope. The first is the key belief about the promise for the future of all believers. I will call this belief *eternity*. The second key belief is in the One who is making the promise. I will simply call this our belief in *God*. Packer suggested I either (1) didn't understand or truly embrace what Christ taught about eternity, or (2) I didn't really understand or trust the One making the promise, namely Jesus.

It didn't take long to pinpoint my answer. What did take a while, however, was to admit the reality to myself, but I finally did. I remember the first time I said it out loud to myself: *"I don't believe in heaven."*

Now, please read this next section carefully before you cast me out as an infidel. I have officiated hundreds of funerals and delivered dozens of sermons on the sweet topic of heaven, believing in my head this is the right answer. But I didn't own the truth in my heart. I wanted to; I just really didn't.

Please know this is a raw but necessary honesty to communicate this premise for us all.

The idea of, in the moment of her death, my mother's spirit exiting her diseased body and going up to heaven to reside with Jesus, along with all those who had gone before — this was just too fantastic an idea for me. I have no mental precedent for such an event. It would certainly help if a few people came back and held a campfire Q&A on the topic. I'm talking not about near-death experiences, but about people who have been gone for a few years and then came back to have a serious conversation or give a presentation about their experience. And since I'm being completely transparent here, living as a disembodied spirit (possibly with wings) and singing worship songs 24/7 forever are just not very appealing ideas to me.

The truth is, if I was given three choices, as in . . .

1. Go to heaven
2. Go to hell
3. Stay on earth and continue to experience life as I'm currently experiencing it

... I would choose #3, by far! I would choose heaven second. Because singing "Kumbaya" for eternity is only slightly more appealing than burning in fire.

All right, I said it. I admitted my struggle with eternal hope. Now what? Because I was the senior pastor of a large church, I felt I should share this with my congregation. Bad idea.

I found out that church is a good place to confess what you *believe*, but not a good place to confess your *unbelief*. One woman, a leader in the community and a member of another church, went to the elders and suggested I resign or take a long sabbatical. The truth is, I never felt more spiritually alive. There is something quite liberating about entering a raw dialogue with God, just like the psalmist did. Not only can God handle it; he invites it! Most churches — well, not so much.

We need to give Christians today the same opportunity Jesus gave the centurion who said, "I do believe some things; help me with what I don't believe" (Mark 9:24, my paraphrase). I don't think we'll ever see a vibrant revival in Christianity until we create safe places for Christians to confess their unbelief, because the true heart confession of what we don't believe is the only path to true belief in our hearts.

Many who grow up in the church hit a crisis of unbelief in their teen years. Because a lot of Christian parents and church leaders can't bear to hear about doubt swimming around in their children's minds, too often young people keep doubt to themselves. This faith dilemma can also become magnified during their early years of life at a university. In the silence, little by little, we lose them. Unspoken struggles morph into reasons to no longer believe. The pattern — when they leave home, they also eventually leave their faith.

Instead, we should invite this confession of unbelief. In my experience, the journey of belief from head to heart is almost always coupled with and fueled by a season of doubt in which a young adult is making a decision to embrace or reject the faith of their parents. We need to create an environment in the home and the church where they are encouraged to speak their doubts out loud. When they do, our response should be, "Great! We were looking forward to this day." With the mouth being halfway from the head to the heart, the confession of unbelief or doubt means the teen or young adult is also halfway home to truly owning their personal faith.

Act Like Jesus—PRACTICES

Now what should I do? I can't get stuck here. Time to *act like Jesus.* This is where *spiritual practices* and disciplines enter in, such as worship, prayer, Bible study, engaging in community, offering my resources, and sharing my faith.

In his book *The Spirit of the Disciplines*, Dallas Willard introduced me to an important principle: *Spiritual practices are the exercises engaged in with the Spirit, whereby we slowly move a truth of God from our head to our heart.*[5]

Even spiritual disciplines designed to serve others turn around and minister to us. The perpetual act reinforces the validity of a biblical belief and gives us an experience with the power of the truth, not just with book knowledge.

Recent research reveals that the number one Christian practice to catalyze spiritual growth is *Bible engagement*, with no close second.[6] This is where I began in my quest for hope.

I opened the Bible with a fresh perspective to discover God's vision for eternity, for the future on which one builds hope. No denominational ax to grind and no sermon to prepare. This was deeply personal. I was on a treasure hunt to discover and experience lasting hope made available to me through Christ.

Five fresh discoveries resulted. Since I have a degree in theology and another in biblical studies, you may think I would have had these down pat — but I didn't. I knew about them, but their collective reality had not yet settled in.

Discovery #1: God isn't finished when we die. He takes care of us and holds on to us, but there is still more to come. All the really good stuff starts unfolding at the return of Christ. Now it makes sense that John would end the last book of the Bible with the phrase, "Come, Lord Jesus" (Revelation 22:20). John had been given an IMAX 3D audiovisual encounter with what is to come and wanted to hurry up and get there. Maybe if I had seen what he saw, I would have voiced the same prayer.

Discovery #2: The end place is not *up there*, but *down here*. God is going to do what he did in Genesis 1 – 2 all over again. The first two chapters of the Bible bear an uncanny resemblance to the last two chapters of the Bible. God is going to create "a new heaven and a new earth" (Revelation 21:1). We will live on the new earth — a very real place. I now have a mental model for this paradigm. As I am writing this chapter, I am on a cruise ship sailing from Belize back to Houston. The sun is bright; the water is blue; and the breeze is gentle. Just yesterday, I was with my wife, son, and daughter-in-law in a magnificent rain forest on the island of Roatán in Honduras. We are heading home to the beautiful hill country north of San Antonio, Texas, where God did some of his finest work. While I love earth living, I believe God can do again what he once did — remove all the bad stuff — and I am ready to make the jump right now. Come quickly, Lord Jesus!

Discovery #3: God is not staying *up there*, but he is coming *down here* to be with us, like he did with Adam and Eve, to take walks in the cool of the day (see Genesis 3:8). I feel the presence of God in my life — I really do. I pray almost nonstop. However, having God actually here with us is a dramatic improvement, if you ask me.

Discovery #4: We are going to receive new bodies — imperishable ones. No more disease, and no more death. I don't know about you, but I am also hoping for a few other modifications — a little divine "nip and tuck" here and there.

Discovery #5: The garden, from which Adam and Eve were escorted away, is at the center of a grand new city. The garden has been expanded, however, to accommodate the number of residents. Let me share the description from John's vision:

> Then I saw "a new heaven and a new earth," for the first heaven and the first earth had passed away, and there was no longer any sea. I saw the Holy City, the new Jerusalem, coming down out of heaven from God, prepared as a bride beautifully dressed for her husband. And I heard a loud voice from the throne saying, "Look! God's dwelling place is now among the people, and he will dwell with them. They will be his people, and God himself will be with them and be their God. 'He will wipe every tear from their eyes. There will be no more death' or mourning or crying or pain, for the old order of things has passed away."
>
> He who was seated on the throne said, "I am making everything new!" (Revelation 21:1–5).

Let's keep reading a bit further:

> Then the angel showed me the river of the water of life, as clear as crystal, flowing from the throne of God and of the Lamb down the middle of the great street of the city. On each side of the river stood the tree of life, bearing twelve crops of fruit, yielding its fruit every month. And the leaves of the tree are for the healing of the nations. No longer will there be any curse. The throne of God and of the Lamb will be in the city, and his servants will serve him. They will see his face, and his name will be on their foreheads. There will be no more night. They will not need the light of a lamp or the light of the sun, for the Lord God will give them light. And they will reign for ever and ever (Revelation 22:1–5).

A river containing not just water but the water of life — clear as crystal — flowing from the throne of God. Now, this just might be something to see! This river flows right down the middle of the street. On each side of the water is a tree — not just any variety of tree, mind you, but the tree of life from the original garden of

Eden, bearing fruit to give eternal life. This could be magnificent and quite helpful — free and unlimited access to the fruit of the tree Adam and Eve ignored. We bite into it, and it has an amazing taste. We notice a *hint* of eternity with every bite.

The tree of the knowledge of good and evil is nowhere to be found. We made our choice on the old earth, and now this tree has no purpose. The serpent has been locked up forever, no longer having access to the garden. Yay, God!

And then it dawned on me. This great river flowing from the throne of God will certainly rival Niagara Falls. So it turns out the trip with my mother has not been canceled after all, but just postponed. And the trip is paid for in full, not by her son, but by the Son of God. And my mother will not be able to wiggle out of this one by dying. Death has been thrown into the lake of fire, never to bother us again.

I don't really get disembodied spirits floating on clouds, getting angels' wings, or working to earn them, like Clarence in *It's a Wonderful Life*. But I do get this vision and also now want it. I really think, from my heart, Jesus was telling us the truth about this eternity, this hope of heaven.

I believe . . . I believe!

I believe from my heart that the vision is true, because I believe the One who makes the promise is trustworthy. He has gone on ahead to prepare a place for us — not a few days in a rented hotel room facing the falls, but a permanent place by the river of life.

So while we wait in hope as he prepares a place for us, he is also *preparing us for that place*. He's pruning us, working in us and on us, and I am grateful he is.

You know, God wants to prune you as well, if only you will let him. He wants to work in you to create a deeper work. God doesn't do this to pick on you or to pay you back for being bad. He has a vision for you to become like Jesus. This is truly the best way to get the most out of this life. Our good God wants this for you and for me. For our own sake? Sure. But the real motivation of a life of love is "for the sake of others." Your family and friends will benefit greatly from tasting the fruit of your life produced by the Spirit. A bouquet of love, joy, and peace; an aroma of patience, kindness, goodness, and faithfulness; a hint of gentleness, self-control, hope, and humility.

I have discovered over my forty years of following Christ that I am often willing to shortchange myself on experiencing the best he offers me. Maybe I don't feel like I deserve it. Maybe I am just okay with settling for the status quo. However, when it comes to becoming like Jesus for the benefit of my wife, four children, grandchildren, neighbors, and others, I find great motivation. I want to do my part to provide the kind of community God envisioned for us when he created us in the first place. I want to pay forward what he has first given to me. I want to love because he first loved me (see 1 John 4:19).

If you have any interest in this kind of life, this book is for you. As you turn the page to part 1, you will begin your journey in the ten key beliefs of *thinking like Jesus*. The goal is to renew your mind in these key truths found throughout the pages of the Bible.

In part 2, we will probe the ten key practices of the Christian life. Here you will be invited to the adventure of *acting like Jesus*. Engaging in spiritual disciplines not only aids us in expressing devotion to God and love for our neighbors; it also helps us move the key beliefs from our head to our heart.

Then, in part 3, we will take a close look at each of the ten key virtues. Possessing these qualities "in increasing measure," as Peter invites us to pursue them, will move us inch by inch, day by day, toward *becoming more like Jesus* (2 Peter 1:8). And living like Jesus is absolutely the best way to live — now and forever.

In part 4, the attention is turned toward you. My heartfelt desire is that one day you will tell your own story, just as I have in this introduction. As people "read your story," mostly revealed in the way you live differently in their presence, they will also want to think, act, and be more like Jesus. This is the goal of this book and of the Christian life. Nothing more; nothing less.

If we never meet each other in this life, I look forward to seeing you in the next. You will be able to find me by the great river. Stop by. I would love to introduce you to my mom.

PART 1

Think Like Jesus
What Do I Believe?

Just as you received Christ Jesus as Lord, continue to live your lives in him, rooted and built up in him, strengthened in the faith as you were taught, and overflowing with thankfulness.

See to it that no one takes you captive through hollow and deceptive philosophy, which depends on human tradition and the elemental spiritual forces of this world rather than on Christ.

COLOSSIANS 2:6–8

When Christ saves us and we are grafted into his vine and ushered into his kingdom, the Spirit of God, the presence of God, comes to live within our hearts. He is now the center of our lives. Christ is, so to speak, the hub of the wheel, now creating movement in us, for him.

Every thought, action, and virtue produced from our renewed and redeemed mind and heart is born from and empowered by the very presence of God. He is the origin and catalyst for this mighty momentum available in our lives.

We begin this individual revolution, this spiritual rotation, with thinking like Jesus, with believing like Jesus.

So we must begin by asking, "What are the key beliefs of Christianity that, when embraced in the mind and the heart, create true change in our individual lives, in the church, and in the world?"

Throughout the history of the church, thoughtful students of Scripture have identified the biggest ideas. These central beliefs have unified and empowered the church over the centuries. While there are multiple views within each of these topics, there is a body of truth all Christians embrace. This unifying content draws together followers of Jesus from all times, all ages, and all places on our globe.

Over the course of the next ten chapters, we'll focus on the top ten key beliefs of the Christian life.[7] While a myriad of beliefs and truths are presented in the Bible, these beliefs are, in my opinion (and based on my aforementioned work with Packer, Willard, and Gallup), the top ten themes affecting our spiritual development. Within each topic, we will address three areas:

1. **KEY QUESTION:** What life question does this belief answer?

2. **KEY IDEA:** What is the unifying concept of this belief that most Christians embrace?[8]

3. **KEY APPLICATION:** What difference does this make in the way I live?

Your first goal is to read each belief to *understand* it. Once you do, you need to ask yourself honestly if you then also *believe*. Do you believe it enough to take such truth down deep into your heart? If the answer is yes, the remaining step is to simply *live it* from the power source of God's presence in your life.

God

May the grace of the Lord Jesus Christ, and the love of
God, and the fellowship of the Holy Spirit be with you all.

2 CORINTHIANS 13:14

A little girl in kindergarten was drawing a picture when her teacher
walked up to her desk to take a look. She asked the child, "What
are you drawing?" The bright-eyed girl quickly responded, "God."
The teacher smiled and then said, "Well, honey, no one actually
knows what God looks like." The child looked up from her work
and confidently quipped, "Well then, they're about to!"

This little girl had no doubts at all as to whether God exists;
rather, she was now going to show the world what he looked like to
her. This is exactly where we must begin in examining our belief
in God — not with, "Does he exist?" but with, "Who is he?"

Theologian A. W. Tozer wrote, "What comes into our minds
when we think about God is the most important thing about us."[9]
Why? Because this mind-set — or absence of it — will drive all we
are and all we do.

KEY QUESTION: Who is God?

Any discussion or teaching regarding this big idea will have to
start with the question, "Who is God?" The Bible's very first words
are, "In the beginning God ..." (Genesis 1:1). Our very lives, as a
part of this creation story, also begin with God as our Creator.

The story of the world's beginning has no hint of defense. No language flirting with a desire to prove. No attempt to allow for anything other than this overarching truth being true. The entire Bible from Genesis to Revelation is written on the assumption there is a God — the constant focal character of each story.

The apostle Paul writes, "For since the creation of the world God's invisible qualities — his eternal power and divine nature — have been clearly seen, being understood from what has been made, so that people are without excuse" (Romans 1:20).

From Gallup's first poll in 1944 to its 2011 poll, Americans who believe in God have stayed inside the 90th-percentile range. Though declining somewhat, the affirmative answer has stayed strong as an overwhelming majority.[10]

So our central question here is not, "Is there a God?" but "Who is the one true God?"

Joshua 24 describes a powerful moment when Israel's leader calls all the tribes together. Joshua is coming to the end of his life and wants to challenge the people to stay true to the God of Abraham, Isaac, and Jacob. After he rehearses God's powerful intervention on their behalf and his protection of them, he offers this challenge:

> "Now fear the LORD and serve him with all faithfulness. Throw away the gods your ancestors worshiped beyond the Euphrates River and in Egypt, and serve the LORD. But if serving the LORD seems undesirable to you, then choose for yourselves this day whom you will serve, whether the gods your ancestors served beyond the Euphrates, or the gods of the Amorites, in whose land you are living. But as for me and my household, we will serve the LORD" (Joshua 24:14 – 15).

Scripture makes it clear that there have always been, and will always be, other gods that people choose to follow. God freely talks about his competition, if you will, for our attention. He allows us the choice.

Here is the declaration God wants us to make:

KEY IDEA: I believe the God of the Bible is the only true God— Father, Son, and Holy Spirit.

Throughout the Old Testament, the clarion call is for belief in the oneness of God. The *Shema* (Hebrew for "hear") forms the belief without mincing words: "Hear, O Israel: The LORD our God, the LORD is one" (Deuteronomy 6:4). Judaism and the Christian faith are rooted in monotheism—one God. This idea stood in radical contrast to all the other religions of the day. Israel's neighbors had come to accept scores of gods, each with their own influence, limitations, and petty self-interests.

Yet, as we turn the page to the New Testament, the names of what seem to be three deities emerge—each declaring to be God—God the Father, God the Son, and God the Holy Spirit. These three are mentioned and appear throughout the Old Testament era, but their distinctive identity and presence invade the life and times of the New Testament.

In 2 Corinthians 13:14, Paul addresses the three persons in one sentence: "May the grace of the Lord Jesus Christ, and the love of God, and the fellowship of the Holy Spirit be with you all."

At Jesus' baptism, we see all three present simultaneously, playing a role in the work of redemption.

"As soon as Jesus was baptized, he went up out of the water. At that moment heaven was opened, and he saw the Spirit of God descending like a dove and alighting on him. And a voice from heaven said, 'This is my Son, whom I love; with him I am well pleased'" (Matthew 3:16–17).

How do we reconcile this mathematical equation of 3 = 1? Throughout church history, clarity developed on what this did not mean:

- God is not three separate gods (tritheism; modern-day Mormonism)

- God is not one God who manifests himself in different roles or modes (modalism; Oneness Pentecostalism)

- Jesus is not subordinate to God the Father (subordinationism; modern-day Jehovah's Witness)

Yet there is something about the nature of God we are missing. Theologians invented the word *Trinity* (a word not used in the Bible) to capture God's essence — three persons who share a being, or fundamental nature. Throughout the centuries, students of the Bible have come up with analogies to get at the heart of the nature of God as a Trinity and to make it a more accessible and practical concept. The following analogy has helped me in developing a practical concept for the nature of God and in understanding what it means to be made in God's image. Of course, all analogies regarding the Trinity fail or break down at some level, so hold this one lightly. But I hope this offers a strong visual for you, as it has for me.

Christians embrace the doctrine of the Trinity as bedrock to our faith. However, not all Christians have a common understanding. I know not all Christian thinkers will embrace my analogy, and that's okay. I include it because it has helped me immensely to see in my daily life the power and practicality of this elusive doctrine. Give me a chance to explain.

You may think I'm splitting theological hairs, but reflecting on this is important on so many levels. For one, the Bible tells us we were created in the image of God as a community: "Then God said, 'Let us make mankind in our image, in our likeness ... So God created mankind in his own image, in the image of God he created them; male and female he created them" (Genesis 1:26–27).

The one true God — Father, Son, and Holy Spirit — created humans in their image as a community. Look again at the verses above. The image of God is in Adam and Eve together. They are not two separate beings — Eve came out of Adam — yet they are distinct persons who can be addressed individually. And we are told the two have become one (see Genesis 2:24). Our true nature is like God. We were not only created for community; in our original design we are a community. We are; therefore I am.

Of course, our unity as a community was fatally injured when Adam and Eve sinned. Selfishness versus others-ness now reigns in our flesh, making it hard for us to grasp our intended nature. This is what Christ came to restore (see John 17:20 – 26). When we enter a relationship with God through Christ, we are placed in the body of Christ (see 1 Corinthians 12:27). We, though we are many, become one (see Romans 12:4 – 5). Imagine everyone who trusts Christ cramming into a huge hula hoop. This is not the same hula hoop as God, but the rebuilding of the hula hoop of Adam and Eve lost in the garden. Christ is restoring our reflection of the nature of God that was lost in the garden of Eden. Now you can understand why relationships are so important to God. All the principles of the Bible, Jesus said, can be placed under "loving God" or "loving neighbor." Relationship! I invite you to rethink the phrase "love your neighbor as yourself." Maybe in God's design, this means your neighbor is a part of what makes up your complete self.

KEY APPLICATION: What difference does this make in the way I live?

If we actually believe this truth about God, not only in our head (understanding) but also in our heart, how can it guide the way we live?

If we embrace the God of the Bible as the one true God, these principles will direct us:

Because God is God …

- I am not.
- I can be sure he is in charge and in control.
- I want to know and follow his will for my life.

If we embrace the threeness of God as Father, Son, and Holy Spirit, we will observe how they treat each other and seek to emulate these principles in our relationships with each other.[11]

Because I was created in the image of God as, and for, community ...

- I recognize the full personhood of others and respect boundaries.

- I look out for the rights, preferences, and comfort of others.

- I value and enjoy others.

For any situation, relationship, or decision we face, we can resolutely apply these principles to guide us. The results, over time, will lead to blessing in our own souls in the form of fruit such as joy and peace, and we will express our actions outwardly for others to enjoy in the form of fruit such as love and kindness.

———————————————

For almost four decades, this one true God has guided my life. I have no backup plan; for me, it's all on Jesus. To the extent I have been willing to learn about God, and to get to know him and trust him, he has faithfully guided me in this same path of blessing. While I have certainly endured many difficult circumstances throughout my life, he has been my comfort and strength, my Savior and guide, in all things.

So, what do you believe? Who is the one true God? Our understanding of God affects everything else in our life, including how we see ourselves and how we treat others.

Personal God

I lift up my eyes to the mountains —
where does my help come from?
My help comes from the LORD,
the Maker of heaven and earth.
PSALM 121:1 – 2

Once you declare that the God of the Bible is the only true God —
Father, Son, and Holy Spirit — your next question as you view the
world becomes, "Is he good?"

KEY QUESTION: Is God good?

Contrary to the opinion of some, God does not have to be good
to exist. After witnessing a human tragedy, some have concluded,
"I don't believe there is a God. No God would allow bad things to
happen to good people." The Greeks and Romans embraced the
religion of paganism. The pagan gods in no way felt obligated to
be good. If it were to turn out these gods were true gods, it would
be unwise to deny their existence. Their followers worshiped
these pagan gods in an attempt to appease them in the hope they
wouldn't pick on them.

The one true God revealed in the Bible doesn't *have* to be good,
but it turns out he is. And not only is he good; he desires to have a
personal relationship with us.

There are at least two things God is not:

1. Uninvolved in creation with no plan (fatalism). This line of
   reasoning suggests bad things happen in our world because

33

there is no God, and there is no plan. Or if there is a God, he has set the world in such a way that our choices and actions are irrelevant anyway. "Que sera sera." This is the same philosophy behind the famous 1980s bumper sticker, "Stuff Happens" (slightly edited for religious consumption).

2. Involved in creating, yet uninvolved in our lives (deism). Adherents to this way of thinking suggest bad things happen in our world because God created the universe to be like a cosmic watch, wound it up, and then let it run on the natural laws he set in place.

On the contrary, when one reads the Bible from beginning to end, here is the declaration God invites us to make:

KEY IDEA: I believe God is involved in and cares about my daily life.

The psalmist writes in Psalm 121:1 – 2:

> I lift up my eyes to the mountains —
>   where does my help come from?
> My help comes from the LORD,
>   the Maker of heaven and earth.

The writer is in a deep valley in need of help. Where does this person look? Who will help him? The psalmist says he will look up — he will look to the creator of the majestic mountains, who then must assuredly have the ability to lift him up and set him high above this lowly place in which he now finds himself.

Consider these key concepts of the qualities of God:

God is above us (transcendent)

God is great; he is above all; and he is not bound by any of the circumstances or events controlling us. He has created everything, and therefore he has complete authority and is in complete control.

So why does a God who has everything care about me? Why does he care about you? This is the same question the psalmist posed:

> When I consider your heavens,
>   the work of your fingers,
> the moon and the stars,
>   which you have set in place,
> what is mankind that you are mindful of them,
>   human beings that you care for them?
> You have made them a little lower than the angels
>   and crowned them with glory and honor.
> You made them rulers over the works of your hands;
>   you put everything under their feet (Psalm 8:3–6).

As hard as it is to grasp, the answer is quite simple: He cares for us because he chooses to.

God is near (immanent)

While God is above the fray of all the things of life that overwhelm us, he also chooses to draw near to us. He comes down and stoops to our level to meet us where we are. Our great God is able to draw close to us, to care and love at a depth we struggle to grasp. The writer of Psalm 121 continues:

> He will not let your foot slip —
>   he who watches over you will not slumber;
> indeed, he who watches over Israel
>   will neither slumber nor sleep.
> The LORD watches over you —
>   the LORD is your shade at your right hand;
> the sun will not harm you by day,
>   nor the moon by night.
> The LORD will keep you from all harm —
>   he will watch over your life;
> the LORD will watch over your coming and going
>   both now and forevermore (Psalm 121:3–8).

Once we accept the fact that God wants to care for us, we are still left to ponder how he has the capacity to do so. I'm a runner and have been for quite some time. A few years back, my daughter introduced me to a smartphone app called RunKeeper. This app tells me how far I've run, my average time per mile, and my overall times, and it also shows me an overview map of exactly where I have run. If I showed you my history on this app, you would see maps of beaches, mountains, and all kinds of locations and terrains. Even more amazing, RunKeeper not only tracks and records *my* locations; it does so for *ten million* other runners as well. If humans can invent a piece of technology to track the steps of ten million people simultaneously, is it really much more of a stretch to believe a transcendent and immanent God can track six billion of us? But he goes a step further. The app doesn't care about me; God does!

God has a plan (provident)

God is not just near us; he has a plan for our lives from the moment of our creation. The psalmist writes in Psalm 139:16:

> Your eyes saw my unformed body;
>   all the days ordained for me were written in your book
>   before one of them came to be.

And the plan God is working out for those who trust him and follow him is good. The apostle Paul assured the early believers of God's great care over their lives:

> [I am] confident of this, that he who began a good work in you will carry it on to completion until the day of Christ Jesus (Philippians 1:6).

> We know that in all things God works for the good of those who love him, who have been called according to his purpose (Romans 8:28).

These verses are just as true for you and me. God's plan, work, and calling apply to all who follow him today.

KEY APPLICATION: What difference does this make in the way I live?

How can believing this truth about God as a personal and good God — not only in our mind (understanding) but also in our heart — guide the way we live?

God's ways are higher than our ways.

In the book of Isaiah, we find God's comparison of his perspective versus our own. He uses the distance between heaven and earth to teach us the breadth and depth of his being:

> "My thoughts are not your thoughts,
>   neither are your ways my ways,"
>   declares the LORD.
> "As the heavens are higher than the earth,
>   so are my ways higher than your ways
>   and my thoughts than your thoughts" (Isaiah 55:8–9).

We are tempted to make frantic decisions because we can't see our way. We can't see around the next bend in the road. God's ways are higher than our ways, because he is seated above on his throne. When we feel that we don't understand God's instruction in his Word, we must remember that he sees things from above and we don't.

God, who controls nature and history, knows and cares about us.

Throughout the Gospels, Jesus conveyed God's care for his children. In Matthew 6, he gave us the profound encouragement to live a life free of worry and fear, leaning fully on our faith:

> "I tell you, do not worry about your life, what you will eat or drink; or about your body, what you will wear. Is not life more than food, and the body more than clothes? Look at the birds of the air; they do not sow or reap or store away in barns, and yet your

heavenly Father feeds them. Are you not much more valuable than they? Can any one of you by worrying add a single hour to your life?

"And why do you worry about clothes? See how the flowers of the field grow. They do not labor or spin. Yet I tell you that not even Solomon in all his splendor was dressed like one of these. If that is how God clothes the grass of the field, which is here today and tomorrow is thrown into the fire, will he not much more clothe you—you of little faith? So do not worry, saying, 'What shall we eat?' or 'What shall we drink?' or 'What shall we wear?' For the pagans run after all these things, and your heavenly Father knows that you need them" (Matthew 6:25–32).

These words about a loving Father paint a vivid picture of a God who is not out to get us, but rather to redeem us. He is not out to destroy us, but rather to restore us.

God is working out his good plan for our lives.

Be reminded of this encouragement from Scripture: "He who began a good work in you will carry it on to completion until the day of Christ Jesus" (Philippians 1:6).

If we truly believe God is involved in and cares about our daily lives, then we can know every morning as we wake up that his heart is to show us his plan, to include us in his big picture. We can also know that in the tough times God will see us through and draw us ever closer to him. His heart is to keep us close to him, no matter what circumstances we may be walking through.

So, what do you believe? Do you believe God is good? Do you believe he is involved in and cares about your daily life? If the answer is yes, then live each day as though it is true. Ponder the difference this can make in your life.

Salvation

For it is by grace you have been saved, through faith—and this is not from yourselves, it is the gift of God—not by works, so that no one can boast.

EPHESIANS 2:8–9

In the introduction, I shared about the unexpected illness and death of my mother. As we delve into the specific belief of salvation, I begin by telling of an encounter I had with her on the way to the hospital. As a result of this brief discussion, I launched my search of the Scriptures on this foundational point of faith. I'll walk through more specifics here of the soul-searching I detailed in the introduction.

When I knew I had to fly to my parents' home in Ohio to help with my mom, I pulled some strings to get her in on short notice to see one of the best oncologists on the staff at the Cleveland Clinic Hospital. On the morning of the appointment, I had to carry my mom out of the house on my back, because the pain in her lower back was so severe. As my dad drove, I sat on the back bench of their travel van where my mom was lying.

Breaking the silence, she asked me a question. "Randy, do you remember when I went to see your youth pastor at the church to help me with some tough issues I was facing? Do you remember when you got home from school that day and I told you he had led me through a prayer to accept Jesus as my Savior?" I responded, "Do I remember? Mom, it was one of the best days of my life."

Then she asked her next question. "Son, was that enough?" With me being the minister in the family, I knew my mother was asking if the simple prayer she prayed to accept Christ was sufficient to give her a relationship with God and entrance into heaven. My quick response was, "You bet it was, Mom." But then later it hit me. This wasn't just anyone dying, and it wasn't just anybody's eternity — it was *my mother*; it was *her eternity*. I needed to take a fresh look at Scripture. If there was more my mom needed to do, I needed to let her know — and let her know right then!

So, with no denominational ax to grind, without caring what had been taught to me in the past, or worrying about what anyone would think about my questioning, I opened my Bible and took a fresh look at the most important query of life.

KEY QUESTION: How do I have a relationship with God?

My focus came down to five particular passages of Scripture. Each one answered the question explicitly.

PASSAGE #1: Do Good Works

Mark writes in his gospel of Jesus' encounter with a rich man:

> As Jesus started on his way, a man ran up to him and fell on his knees before him. "Good teacher," he asked, "what must I do to inherit eternal life?"
>
> "Why do you call me good?" Jesus answered. "No one is good—except God alone. You know the commandments: 'You shall not murder, you shall not commit adultery, you shall not steal, you shall not give false testimony, you shall not defraud, honor your father and mother.'"
>
> "Teacher," he declared, "all these I have kept since I was a boy."
>
> Jesus looked at him and loved him. "One thing you lack," he said. "Go, sell everything you have and give to the poor, and you will have treasure in heaven. Then come, follow me."

At this the man's face fell. He went away sad, because he had great wealth (Mark 10:17–22).

Here we find our original question: *What must I do to inherit eternal life?* We also see that "Jesus looked at him and loved him." He wasn't trying to trick or belittle the man, but rather was attempting to lead him to the truth. While the focus is often placed on the rich man walking away sad, we should not miss the fact that Jesus invites him to follow him.

Taking this passage at face value, we conclude: If we want to have a relationship with God and have eternal life, then, Jesus says, we need to *do good works.*

We will loop back to revisit this statement — lest anyone be concerned we are emphasizing salvation by works. We are building on a scriptural progression of thought, so please read on.

PASSAGE #2: Believe

John in his gospel tells of Jesus' encounter with Nicodemus:

Now there was a Pharisee, a man named Nicodemus ... He came to Jesus at night and said, "Rabbi, we know that you are a teacher who has come from God ..."

Jesus replied, "Very truly I tell you, no one can see the kingdom of God unless they are born again."

"How can someone be born when they are old?" Nicodemus asked. "Surely they cannot enter a second time into their mother's womb to be born!"

Jesus answered, "Very truly I tell you, no one can enter the kingdom of God unless they are born of water and the Spirit. Flesh gives birth to flesh, but the Spirit gives birth to spirit. You should not be surprised at my saying, 'You must be born again.' ...

"How can this be?" Nicodemus asked ...

For God so loved the world that he gave his one and only Son, that whoever believes in him shall not perish but have eternal life (John 3:1–7, 9, 16).

Jesus was describing the spiritual rebirth God requires and came to offer, along with God's motivation for sending him — love.

Therefore, if we want to have a relationship with God and eternal life, then, Jesus says, we must *believe* in him.

PASSAGE #3: Repent and Be Baptized

The day of Pentecost had come, and 120 disciples were huddled together, confused after Jesus had returned to heaven. As Jesus had promised, the Holy Spirit came and filled them — and the church was born.

> *Then Peter stood up with the Eleven, raised his voice and addressed the crowd: "Fellow Jews and all of you who live in Jerusalem, let me explain this to you; listen carefully to what I say . . .*
>
> *'And everyone who calls on*
> *the name of the Lord will be saved.' " . . .*
>
> *When the people heard this, they were cut to the heart and said to Peter and the other apostles, "Brothers, what shall we do?"*
> *Peter replied, "Repent and be baptized, every one of you, in the name of Jesus Christ for the forgiveness of your sins. And you will receive the gift of the Holy Spirit" (Acts 2:14, 21, 37–38).*

The people heard this amazing message Peter delivered and, much like the rich man Jesus encountered, asked, "Okay, so now what do we do?" But on this day, three thousand people understood and accepted the truth of Christ. They turned around from walking away from God and turned toward him. This is what it means to repent, to turn and go the other way — a 180 of the mind and heart — which begins the process of both transformation and sanctification.

Therefore, if we want to have a relationship with God and have eternal life, then, Peter says, we must call on the name of the Lord. How does one do this? Repent and then be baptized.

PASSAGE #4: Believe and Profess

In his letter to the Romans, Paul writes:

> Brothers and sisters, my heart's desire and prayer to God for the Israelites is that they may be saved. For I can testify about them that they are zealous for God, but their zeal is not based on knowledge. Since they did not know the righteousness of God and sought to establish their own, they did not submit to God's righteousness. Christ is the culmination of the law so that there may be righteousness for everyone who believes (Romans 10:1 – 4).

The Israelites were religious people, but they had the wrong strategy. They were trying to develop a righteousness of their own. They were trying to be good enough, through their works, to deserve a relationship with God. In essence, Paul said, "Works don't work." The only one good enough is God. Jesus is God. Jesus fulfilled all the requirements of the law perfectly. When we believe in him, the righteousness of Christ is transferred to our account. This is the only solution. So how do we pull off this transaction? Paul tells us in Romans 10:9 – 10:

> If you declare with your mouth, "Jesus is Lord," and believe in your heart that God raised him from the dead, you will be saved. For it is with your heart that you believe and are justified, and it is with your mouth that you profess your faith and are saved.

Believe with your heart; profess out loud with your mouth — this brand of confession has to come from the heart (see Luke 6:45). An internal decision of the heart brings an outward demonstration of confession — a very similar concept to "repent and be baptized."

Therefore, if we want to have a relationship with God and have eternal life, then, Paul says, we must *believe and profess.*

PASSAGE #5: Come to Faith by Grace

Paul wrote in his letter to the Ephesians:

> *It is by grace you have been saved, through faith—and this is not from yourselves, it is the gift of God—not by works, so that no one can boast (Ephesians 2:8–9).*

In reality, "faith" is not a separate category from "believe." They come from the same word in the Greek language in which the New Testament is written. Yet here Paul clearly adds fresh insights into the salvation transaction.

The word *grace* means we do not deserve salvation. We are not entitled to it, nor is God obligated to offer it to mankind. Yet he makes us this offer of his righteousness we cannot achieve on our own. To respond, we must express faith in who Jesus is and receive what he has done for us.

But notice the phrase "not by works." Is this not different from where we began—with Jesus' words to the rich man to do good works? This could seem at first glance like a discrepancy or conflict between Paul's and Jesus' instructions. But actually, Jesus knew the young man had never, and could never, keep the law perfectly. Jesus was simply trying to get him to see he couldn't! Jesus' challenge for the rich man to give away his wealth was his way of trying to lovingly lead the young man to say, "But, Jesus, I can't. I have not been able to keep the law, and I don't know how I can. I need you." Jesus was hoping to see this man express faith— which aligns with Paul's words: "by grace … through faith … not by works." If Paul was sitting with us in a coffee shop, trying to bring clarity to this issue, perhaps he'd say something like this: "Our good works do not contribute in any way to coming into a right relationship with God, but they do express and manifest that we do have a relationship with God by grace through faith in Jesus Christ."

Denominations within Christianity often emphasize one of these passages over another as believers try to get to the heart of this important issue. Some believe God chooses or elects us to make this decision. Others see it as a matter of complete free will. For some, the order is different; for others, baptism plays a more prominent and nonnegotiable role in this spiritual transaction. The one thing I am sure of is this: Salvation is from Christ alone, and our acceptance of his gift must genuinely come from the expression of faith from the heart.

All of these verses together form this central truth:

KEY IDEA: I believe a person comes into a right relationship with God by God's grace through faith in Jesus Christ.

Here is the decision a person should make from the heart, placed into a prayer of acceptance to God.

Dear God, I can't, but you can.

I believe in Jesus, who is God. I believe he died and rose from the dead. I place my faith in Christ to make me right with you and give me eternal life. I have no other plan but to have faith and to trust you.

I am doing a 180 today and pointing my life toward you. I will no longer run away from you, but toward you.

Then there comes an outward declaration to the world — a way for us to demonstrate our faith decision: "I profess you with my mouth, out loud for others to know where I stand. And I publicly express my full devotion to you through baptism."

While many things in the Bible are difficult to understand, salvation is not one of them. God made it abundantly clear and profoundly simple: "Salvation is found in no one else, for there is no other name under heaven given to mankind by which we must be saved" (Acts 4:12).

Over the centuries Christians have been unified on what salvation in Christ is not.

- **Salvation is not something we can earn or deserve.** When the Jewish believers tried to add circumcision to the equation, the apostles gathered together in a council and made this unified declaration: "No! We believe it is through grace of our Lord Jesus that we are saved, just as they are" (Acts 15:11).

- **Salvation is not one of many ways.** The apostle John records these words of Jesus: "I am the way and the truth and the life. No one comes to the Father except through me" (John 14:6).

- **Salvation is not unconditional reconciliation for all humans (Universalism).** At the end of time at the final judgment, while it is a nice thought, not everyone makes it into God's eternal kingdom (see Revelation 20:11 – 15).

KEY APPLICATION: What difference does this make in the way I live?

- **We seek to please God because of what he has done for us, not to earn a relationship with him.** The apostle Paul writes, "I have been crucified with Christ and I no longer live, but Christ lives in me. The life I now live in the body, I live by faith in the Son of God, who loved me and gave himself for me" (Galatians 2:20). No matter what troubles I face in this life, they pale in comparison to my salvation for eternity. Paul reminds us not to lose heart: "Though outwardly we are wasting away, yet inwardly we are being renewed day by day. For our light and momentary troubles are achieving for us an eternal glory that far outweighs them all" (2 Corinthians 4:16 – 17).

- **We walk in grace.** In his letter to the Galatians, Paul writes, "Before your very eyes Jesus Christ was clearly portrayed as crucified. I would like to learn just one thing from you: Did you receive the Spirit by the works of the law, or by believing what you heard? Are you so foolish? After beginning by means of the Spirit, are you now trying to finish by means of the flesh?" (Galatians 3:1 – 3).

- **We offer grace to others.** Let us not forget Jesus' parable of the unmerciful servant recorded in Matthew 18:21 – 35. It would be wrong and inconsistent for us to refuse to offer grace and forgiveness to someone else in light of the grace and forgiveness God has shown to us.

I was right when I told my mother that her prayer of faith to Jesus was enough to save her. He is, indeed, enough! How about you? Do you believe this offer of Jesus? Have you received it for yourself? None of the other chapters will matter much unless you embrace the truths found in this one.

The Bible

All Scripture is God-breathed and is useful for teaching, rebuking, correcting and training in righteousness, so that the servant of God may be thoroughly equipped for every good work.

2 TIMOTHY 3:16–17

The story is told of the night the Green Bay Packers lost an away game they were expected to win. After the team took the long bus ride back home, legendary coach Vince Lombardi made the players put their sweaty uniforms back on and march out onto Lambeau Field. The coach huddled them together and held up a pigskin, egg-shaped object high in the air and said, "Gentlemen, this is a football!"

Vince Lombardi knew one of the fundamentals of winning a football game is having a firm grasp of the basics. The same is true of the Christian life. So in the spirit of an unforgettable night in bitterly cold Wisconsin, I hold up a black leather book with onion-skin pages and say to you, "Ladies and gentlemen, this is a Bible!"

Why is this so important? Why so essential?

KEY QUESTION: How can I know God and his will for my life?

Knowing with confidence this book is the Word of God that contains God's truth and will for our lives, and knowing how to read and understand it for ourselves, is as basic to the Christian life as a football is to the game of football.

How do we know such important life matters as:

- who the one true God is
- God's love for us
- our birth into sin and separation from God
- Jesus' payment for our sin to restore us
- the best way to live a successful and productive life
- the truth about the future and God's ultimate redemption of man

The Bible not only claims to give answers to these questions but also invites us to believe and embrace so much more.

KEY IDEA: I believe the Bible is the inspired Word of God that guides my beliefs and action.

We would only want to give this book the right to guide our lives if we truly believed it was from God. This is where we need to start our discovery. There are three big concepts we need to understand, and then we can decide for ourselves whether we think this book is from him.

1. The Bible is inspired—breathed out by God himself

The Bible explicitly makes this claim: "All Scripture is God-breathed" (2 Timothy 3:16).[12]

The compound Greek word the author used for "God-breathed" is *theopneustos*—the same word used to translate the original Hebrew word into Greek in Genesis 2:7, where God *breathed* life into Adam's nostrils. The writer of Hebrews confirms the claim: "The word of God is alive and active" (Hebrews 4:12).

Many books we read are truly inspiring. They stir something special in us. The Bible certainly has proven to be such in this respect, but to say the Bible is inspired is to claim it is much more. This book is from God himself! It is alive — a living organism.

What does this actually mean, and how did the Bible come together?

Contrary to what some may think, the Bible did not fall out of the heavens in a leather cover! Rather, it came to us over a long time through the oversight of God in four phases.

PHASE 1: *Revelation*

This phase simply refers to God's ongoing decision to reveal himself to us. Paul's letter to the Romans tells us God reveals himself to all people *externally through nature*. This is called general revelation. "Since the creation of the world God's invisible qualities — his eternal power and divine nature — have been clearly seen, being understood from what has been made, so that people are without excuse" (Romans 1:20).

God also reveals himself to everyone *internally through our consciences*:

> When Gentiles, who do not have the law, do by nature things required by the law, they are a law for themselves, even though they do not have the law. They show that the requirements of the law are written on their hearts, their consciences also bearing witness, and their thoughts sometimes accusing them and at other times even defending them (Romans 2:14–15).

The internal sense of right and wrong and even the very existence of God himself are written into the code of our conscience.

God also reveals himself *through a specific person at a specific time with a specific message* to communicate from himself. Examples of special revelation are dreams and visitations of angels, as we see in the lives of Mary and Joseph, who were both given these direct messages from God. Through this special mode of revelation, God spoke to the authors who penned the books of the Bible, which leads us to phase 2.

PHASE 2: *Inspiration*

God revealed, or breathed, his message into chosen people to be written down. In the Old Testament, it was predominantly the prophets, while in the New Testament, the apostles. It took forty authors over fourteen hundred years to write down the sixty-six books we call the Bible — all originally scribed on parchment paper in large scrolls.

In his second letter, the apostle Peter writes:

> *Above all, you must understand that no prophecy of Scripture came about by the prophet's own interpretation of things. For prophecy never had its origin in the human will, but prophets, though human, spoke from God as they were carried along by the Holy Spirit (2 Peter 1:20–21).*

PHASE 3: *Transmission*

Transmission refers to the painstaking task in which the individual books were copied down to the scale and detail of classic works of art. Those involved in this process applied so much scrutiny to ensure authenticity was being maintained that one page often took several months to complete. For example, in order to check for accuracy, when a page was completed, the middle word on a page was identified, and positioning was checked against the original. If a word did not match up to the exact spot of the standard, the copy was burned and the work started again.

Today, we do not have any of the original scrolls, but we do have thousands of those copies. If you compare the copies we have of the New Testament with its closest book of antiquity — Homer's *Iliad* — 643 copies of the *Iliad* exist today, while 24,000 known copies of the New Testament exist. The oldest known copy of the *Iliad* is 500 years younger than the original, while the oldest copy of the New Testament is less than 100 years removed from the original.[13]

In the New Testament, only 400 words carry any question as to their original penning, none of which relate to actual doctrine.

This is a 99.9 percent accuracy rate. Scholar Benjamin B. Warfield had this to say after years of studying the development of the New Testament:

> If we compare the present state of the New Testament with that of any other ancient writing, we must ... declare it to be marvelously correct. Such has been the care with which the New Testament has been copied — a care which has doubtless grown out of true reverence for its holy words — such has been the providence of God in preserving for his Church in each and every age a competently exact text of the Scripture, that not only is the New Testament unrivalled among ancient writings in the purity of its text as actually transmitted and kept in use, but also in the abundance of testimony which has come down to us for castigating its comparatively infrequent blemishes.[14]

It is clear from these historical facts that God himself oversaw the handling and care of his Word in a meticulous manner. Factor in the numerous attempts at literary genocide of the Bible, and our confidence in it only rises. After an amazing amount of testing, time, energy, and divine guidance, in AD 400, nearly 370 years after Christ's death, the sixty-six books as we know them today officially came together for the first time under one cover.[15]

PHASE 4: *Translation*

Translation refers to the process by which the Bible was translated from the original Hebrew and Greek copies into other languages. One of the first translations was in Latin and called Jerome's *Biblia Sacra Vulgata*.

Today we have a variety of translations and paraphrases of the Bible, with more in process even as I write. Many ministries are working with people groups all over the world to bring the Bible to the estimated 180 million who do not have Scripture in their own language. To date, only 513 of the more than 7,000 languages in the world have complete Bibles in that native tongue.[16]

After investigating the origins and process throughout history of how this special book came to us, millions of people have come to believe it is the very Word of God. I am definitely one of those people. How about you?

2. The Bible is authoritative—possessing the right to direct our lives

As the Word of God, the Bible has the right to govern a Christian's life. As a result, we cannot treat it as a buffet, where we pick and choose what we read and obey, but rather we must take the entire book as a total work and accept every word. As we swear with our left hand placed on a copy of the Bible in a courtroom, it is "the truth, the whole truth, and nothing but the truth, so help me, God."

The longest psalm in the Bible celebrates the Word of God and its authoritative nature:

> Blessed are those whose ways are blameless,
>   who walk according to the law of the LORD.
> Blessed are those who keep his statutes
>   and seek him with all their heart—
> they do no wrong
>   but follow his ways.
> You have laid down precepts
>   that are to be fully obeyed (Psalm 119:1–4).

3. The Bible is infallible—unfailing in accomplishing its purposes

The prophet Isaiah writes in Isaiah 55:10–11:

> As the rain and the snow
>   come down from heaven,
> and do not return to it
>   without watering the earth
> and making it bud and flourish,
>   so that it yields seed for the sower and bread for the eater,

so is my word that goes out from my mouth:
   It will not return to me empty,
but will accomplish what I desire
   and achieve the purpose for which I sent it.

What God's Word says will come about, *will* come about. What God's Word says it will do in our life, it *will* do in our life.

KEY APPLICATION: What difference does this make in the way I live?

If someone actually believed this about the Bible from their heart, how would they live differently?

- **The Bible is the lens from which we view the world.** Every one of us sees the world and each day unfold through a set of lenses. When we look over our shoulder, these spectacles form an image in our mind of the past. As we squint to see as far as the eye can see, these lenses will give us a vision of the future. God's Word informs what we think and feel about everything we encounter. We see the intervention of God in history, in our present lives, and on into the future as he continues to write his grand story.

- **We are obligated and motivated to study the Bible to understand God's will for our lives.** The apostle Paul wrote, "Do not conform to the pattern of this world, but be transformed by the renewing of your mind. Then you will be able to test and approve what God's will is — his good, pleasing and perfect will" (Romans 12:2). The Bible forms the content of truth we seek to marinate our minds in. We seek to do as the psalmist suggests: "I meditate on it all day long" (Psalm 119:97).

- **The principles in the Bible must govern our lives, even when we don't fully understand or like what they teach us.** In the book of Proverbs, we find this wise command: "Trust in the LORD with all your heart and lean not on your own understanding; in all your ways submit to him, and he will make your paths straight" (Proverbs 3:5 – 6).

Renowned theologian Søren Kierkegaard challenges our false front: "The Bible is very easy to understand. But we Christians are a bunch of scheming swindlers. We pretend to be unable to understand it because we know very well that the minute we understand, we are obliged to act accordingly."[17]

The writer of Hebrews tells us the Bible is "sharper than any double-edged sword" and "penetrates even to dividing soul and spirit, joints and marrow; it judges the thoughts and attitudes of the heart" (Hebrews 4:12). Put another way, its words have a way of getting under our skin.

The Bible is not a book of suggestions, but rather claims to be the very Word of God and invites you to let it rule and guide every aspect of your life. So, are you in or out?

Do you believe the Bible is the Word of God and that it has the right to command your belief and action?

Identity in Christ

Yet to all who did receive him, to those who believed in his
name, he gave the right to become children of God.

JOHN 1:12

At 4:48 a.m. on October 3, 1987, Rozanne and I had our second
child. It had been a long night of pushing and coaching. To top it
off, I had flu-like symptoms. When David finally emerged, I was
overjoyed. We already had a girl, but now we had a boy. *Life is perfect and complete*, I thought. Then I looked down and noticed our
son's left arm — everything below his elbow was missing!

I apparently turned white as a ghost, causing the nurses to
usher me out of the room. They directed me to a stainless steel
sink in case I needed to stick my head in it and throw up. I didn't
get sick, but I did have a bunch of questions and thoughts swimming through my head.

What about playing baseball with my son?

What about his first day in kindergarten, and the painful feelings that would bring?

What about the mean kids in junior high school tearing down
an easy mark to build themselves up?

What about on his wedding day when the minister — most
likely me — asks his bride to repeat her vows to my son, while she
places the ring on his wedding finger? *He doesn't have one. It won't
matter; what girl will want a boy who's missing a hand?*

The final question poured into my head involuntarily: "Will I
love him?" *I had wanted and expected a different outcome. Will I
be able to accept my son the same way I do my daughter?*

I am not sure how much time passed as the questions flooded my mind, but eventually a nurse came back to get me. When I reentered the delivery room, another nurse was holding my son, and he was wrapped in a warm blanket. She handed David to me, and I held him. I loved him! He was my son. It suddenly became so simple.

One of the most important indicators of your happiness and quality of life will come from the answer to this key question.

KEY QUESTION: Who am I?

If you like your answer to this question, you have a good foundation on which to build your life. If you hate your answer to this question, it is not going to go well with you. If you aren't sure yet, this will help.

Here is Jesus' answer to you and for you ...

KEY IDEA: I believe I am significant because of my position as a child of God.

Psychology tells us some of the major factors necessary to have a healthy self-esteem are:

- to feel loved
- to have a sense of purpose
- to feel secure
- to feel significant
- to have a sense of belonging

If we believe God to be who he claims to be, then it is safe to say he is "The Ultimate Somebody." Along with what we've declared thus far in this chapter, we also may believe we have been accepted and adopted by "The Ultimate Somebody" and now gain our identity, love, purpose, security, significance, and belonging in and through him.

The words of Scripture remind us that we are welcomed into God's family as his children:

To all who did receive him, to those who believed in his name, he gave the right to become children of God (John 1:12).

See what great love the Father has lavished on us, that we should be called children of God! And that is what we are! (John 3:1).

If my love for my son David can be so true and deep, how much more is this true about God's love for us, his children?

A second important question to ask is, "Whose voice am I listening to?" The answer to this question significantly impacts our view of who we are.

Often, the voice being heard today echoes from our past, possibly from decades ago. Maybe words from ...

- an abusive parent
- a belligerent employer
- a bitter ex-spouse
- a belittling boyfriend or girlfriend
- a bullying coach
- a small-town gossip
- a rejection letter
- an online comment

Or maybe the voice you hear is not a human one, but an inaudible scream from a scene you keep viewing. Maybe it's ...

- the cover of *Success* magazine
- the address down the street where the Joneses live
- the image on the computer or TV screen
- the reflection in the mirror every morning

We must identify the voice (or voices) telling us who we are. The great news is that no matter to whom we have listened, or for how long, God wants to tell us exactly who we are. The moment we profess faith in him, we receive a new identity. Each day, God's voice will not only whisper to us that we are his, but it will also silence the voices that for far too long have lied to us about who we are. But just as so many of us have repeated the lies we eventually believed, we can start to continually listen to God and repeat who we are in him so we can believe his truth and act on it.

As a believer in Jesus Christ, you are a child of God and heir to his kingdom.

> *If we are children, then we are heirs—heirs of God and co-heirs with Christ, if indeed we share in his sufferings in order that we may also share in his glory (Romans 8:17).*

Our time on earth is to be spent loving our Father and building his kingdom, which he freely shares with us — now and in eternity. He has given us full access to himself, his character, his gifts, and his qualities.

As a believer in Jesus Christ, you are a temple of God's dwelling.

> *Don't you know that you yourselves are God's temple and that God's Spirit dwells in your midst? (1 Corinthians 3:16).*

Being the temple for God's dwelling shines an entirely new light and responsibility on taking care of our bodies, minds, and spirits. Our new motive in caring for ourselves is not to be loved and accepted by people on the outside, but rather to care for ourselves because of God, who lives on the inside. This also challenges and inspires us in our daily behavior, because we now take God with us everywhere we go.

As a believer in Jesus Christ, you are a new creation.

> *If anyone is in Christ, the new creation has come: The old has gone, the new is here! (2 Corinthians 5:17).*

God sees us as totally different beings — new creations — because of his Son, who now resides in our souls. One day, as promised in the book of Revelation, God will start over with a new heaven and a new earth — and all we will see, and know, is the new! Until then, let us start seeing ourselves as God sees us, and living up to his vision for us, starting today.

As a believer in Jesus Christ, you are a member of the body of Christ.

Now you are the body of Christ, and each one of you is a part of it (1 Corinthians 12:27).

As a member of the body of Christ, you now belong to the largest family in existence. You have a seat at God's table, and one day you will sit at his table in full view of Christ himself. This great family, led by our Father, gives us a unique sense of eternal purpose and calling. Our talents and gifts take on significant meanings to the people around us, as well as to the kingdom as a whole. There is no greater purpose than to be associated with the purposes of God through his body, his family. Paul likens this connecting concept to a growing and maturing physical body:

Speaking the truth in love, we will grow to become in every respect the mature body of him who is the head, that is, Christ. From him the whole body, joined and held together by every supporting ligament, grows and builds itself up in love, as each part does its work (Ephesians 4:15 – 16).

As a believer in Jesus Christ, you are a citizen of heaven.

Our citizenship is in heaven. And we eagerly await a Savior from there, the Lord Jesus Christ (Philippians 3:20).

I have a passport. It contains my name, address, and picture, but most importantly, it is an official document that tells anyone in the world I am a citizen of the United States. I can go to any foreign country, but I'm always freely allowed back into the U.S., because my citizenship is located here. The passport is my proof.

As followers of Christ and citizens of heaven, it does not matter what nation we are from, what race we are, or what our income level or IQ is, for when the day of the Lord comes, we have access through the gates of heaven because Jesus has officially declared us free to pass into his kingdom. This is where I belong! The indwelling Spirit — the one in whom we are marked with a seal — is our passport (see Ephesians 1:13 – 14).

We now have a higher standard, because we are called not only to abide by the laws of the land, but also to adhere to the laws of heaven. If Christians will walk in obedience to both, we will impact the world more deeply for Christ.

KEY APPLICATION: What difference does this make in the way I live?

If you truly embrace in your heart your new identity in Christ, a significant difference will be seen in the way you approach each day.

Because of our new identity in Christ, we are free from condemnation.

> *What a wretched man I am! Who will rescue me from this body that is subject to death? Thanks be to God, who delivers me through Jesus Christ our Lord!*
>
> *So then, I myself in my mind am a slave to God's law, but in my sinful nature a slave to the law of sin*
>
> *Therefore, there is now no condemnation for those who are in Christ Jesus, because through Christ Jesus the law of the Spirit who gives life has set you free from the law of sin and death* (Romans 7:24 – 8:2).

Many people struggle with accepting God's grace and mercy. But Paul's declaration of "no condemnation" means judgment, accusation, and bondage to sin are no more. We must believe in the work of Christ and walk into his freedom.

When Satan tries to condemn us, Jesus acts as our advocate, our attorney. He stands before the Father to say, "I object. They have already been acquitted of these charges" (see Romans 8:34).

When another human tries to tell you that you are insignificant or treat you like you are worthless, don't listen to them. In Christ, this is simply not true.

Because of our new identity in Christ, our worth comes from our position in Christ, not our performance.

"Come to me, all you who are weary and burdened, and I will give you rest. Take my yoke upon you and learn from me, for I am gentle and humble in heart, and you will find rest for your souls" (Matthew 11:28–29).

Notice Jesus is not talking just about being physically tired, because he expressly says, "You will find rest for your *souls.*" It is exhausting work to try to prove our worth and perform to gain significance, and it causes us to be "weary and burdened." Christ alone offers the freedom from the tyranny of any demands for approval. He gives us a place at his table — secure in our position in him because of who he is and what he has done for us.

Because of our new identity in Christ, we live to express who we are in Christ, not to prove who we are.

One of my favorite movies is the 1981 Academy Award-winning film *Chariots of Fire*, which tells the true story of Eric Liddell and Harold Abrahams. Liddell, a Christian Scotsman, and Abrams, a Jew, both ran in the 1924 Olympics. The movie depicts how they both ran and won gold medals. The difference? Harold Abrahams ran to prove who he was, while Eric Liddell ran to express who he knew he was in Christ.

There is a scene in which Liddell's sister is deeply concerned because she senses that his running is pulling him away from their commitment to go to China as missionaries. He looks deep into his sister's eyes and says, "I believe God made me for a purpose, but he also made me fast. And when I run, I feel his pleasure." Eric ran in the Olympics, and yet he later went on to serve the Lord in China.

One of the most mystical, yet amazing ways we know we are truly expressing who we are in Christ is by using the gifts he gives and tapping into the heart of God to "feel his pleasure," as Liddell poetically described it. It's feeling deep down that this kingdom activity I'm engaged in is a gift from my Creator and the reason I'm on this planet.

Because of our new identity in Christ, we can focus on building others up, not tearing them down.

If anyone acknowledges that Jesus is the Son of God, God lives in them and they in God. And so we know and rely on the love God has for us.

God is love. Whoever lives in love lives in God, and God in them. This is how love is made complete among us so that we will have confidence on the day of judgment: In this world we are like Jesus (1 John 4:15–17).

The more we know and accept who we are in Christ, the more our behavior will begin to reflect our true identity. It will translate into not allowing anyone or anything to devalue who we are in Christ.

We will be set free to use our words for building bridges, not burning them. To use our hands to hug, not hurt. To use our feet to bring to, not take away. To use our hearts to inspire, not conspire. To raise the level of any room we are in, not bring it down.

As we love God and grow deeper in our love for him, we will then, anywhere and everywhere we go, be Jesus with skin on. This is truly thinking like Jesus!

Our son David is now twenty-six years old. As it turned out, he played every sport imaginable — more than I ever did, and with better results. He was all-conference in football. Numerous articles were written about him, and Fox aired a wonderful segment on his athletic accomplishments. He is married to a beautiful and intelligent Christian journalist. He is an attorney with a major firm in Indianapolis. Most of all, David is a modern-day Eric Liddell. He knows who he is in Christ, and he runs each day to express himself versus trying to prove who he is. A little of this mind-set has even rubbed off on his dad.

So let me ask you: If you have received Christ as your Savior, do you believe and rest in your new identity in him? If not, why not? When you received Christ, such a decision wasn't just meant for the age to come; it was meant to give you a life of immense freedom and rest now as well. Grab hold of it!

Church

Speaking the truth in love, we will grow to become
in every respect the mature body of him who is the
head, that is, Christ.

EPHESIANS 4:15

In John 14:11 – 13, Jesus made an interesting yet perplexing
statement:

> *"Believe me when I say that I am in the Father and the Father
> is in me; or at least believe on the evidence of the works them-
> selves. Very truly I tell you, whoever believes in me will do the
> works I have been doing, and they will do even greater things
> than these, because I am going to the Father. And I will do what-
> ever you ask in my name, so that the Father may be glorified in
> the Son."*

As his followers, we will do the same things Jesus did. What
a tall order! But then we "will do even greater things than these"?
Greater? How could we possibly do this?

Years ago, an issue of *Proceedings of the National Academy
of Science* reported that a supercolony of ants was discovered,
stretching thousands of miles from the Italian Riviera along the
coastline to northwest Spain. This was the largest cooperative unit
ever recorded, according to Swiss, French, and Danish scientists
who studied the phenomenon. The colony consisted of billions of
Argentine ants living in millions of nests and cooperating with
one another. Normally, ants from different nests will fight, but the

researchers concluded the ants in this particular supercolony were close enough genetically to recognize one another.

Laurent Keller of the University of Lausanne, Switzerland, summed it up: "Cooperation allowed the colonies to develop at much higher densities than would normally occur ... This led to the greatest cooperative unit ever discovered."[18]

Individually, we can never do "greater things" than Jesus, yet just like those early followers we read about in the book of Acts, who worked in cooperation and recognition among their brothers and sisters, we can indeed accomplish his works in great volume across the street and around the world.

KEY QUESTION: How does God accomplish his purposes today?

In the Old Testament, God was in an ongoing relationship with the nation of Israel to reveal his name, his identity, and his plan to the nations. Every account written regarding Israel was intended to point people to the first coming of Jesus. But after Christ came to earth, did the work the Father sent him to do, died on the cross, defeated sin and death through the resurrection, and returned to heaven, God commissioned a new community. A convergence of Jews and Gentiles sharing in a new life together, as a family called the church.

The Bible teaches us this church is the primary — yet not exclusive — method to be used in accomplishing God's purposes on into eternity. Today, a vital mission in this body of believers is to point people toward the *second* coming of Christ.

The person who embraces salvation by grace, as we discussed in the Salvation belief section, is inducted and integrated into the church as a full member.

While it is true a person expressing faith in Christ can gain salvation and never become an active member in God's church, this absence of community will create a hindrance not unlike a train with no track or a car with no wheels. The identity may be in place, but there's no purpose to the existence.

KEY IDEA: I believe the church is God's primary way to accomplish his purposes on earth.

In 1 Corinthians 12:12 – 14, Paul uses language regarding the human body to describe how the body of Christ works to function and find its purpose:

> Just as a body, though one, has many parts, but all its many parts form one body, so it is with Christ. For we were all baptized by one Spirit so as to form one body—whether Jews or Gentiles, slave or free—and we were all given the one Spirit to drink. Even so the body is not made up of one part but of many.

Since any belief system is always just one generation away from extinction, we must ask how we are doing today in becoming what Paul describes here. Over the past few decades, we've seen a strong trend of young people walking away from the church when they left their parents' home and their home church. But we've also seen many coming back into the fold after "settling down" to family and career. Today we see a new trend — leaving and not coming back.

Certainly we would all admit that the church far too often doesn't look the way Christ intends it to look. In fact, many today readily confess to not really having a problem with Jesus as much as with his bride, the church. And then there are those in our fast-paced, breakneck-speed culture who struggle to be a part of church, because they just can't add one more activity to their life list, especially if they no longer see the relevance in the time investment.

But trends and statistics aside, in light of God's commands regarding his body, there are tremendous benefits in being a part of the church—the great community of believers who are daily advancing his kingdom.

KEY APPLICATION: What difference does this make in the way I live?

In the body of Christ, you belong to a family focused on all the things of God, which are good, right, and healthy.

Paul writes these words in his letter to the Philippians:

> *Brothers and sisters, whatever is true, whatever is noble, whatever is right, whatever is pure, whatever is lovely, whatever is admirable—if anything is excellent or praiseworthy—think about such things. Whatever you have learned or received or heard from me, or seen in me—put it into practice. And the God of peace will be with you (Philippians 4:8–9).*

As a pastor, I have met with countless people who struggle with church. As we talk and delve into their lives, I typically find one of two things. First, they have never truly been a part of this level of community and relationship, so they don't understand what is available and can be added to their lives. Simply put, you can't fully know what you're missing if you've never experienced it. Second, a community they've been a part of in the past tore them down and caused hurt. Even if they had contributed to the conflict, the experience created a physical and emotional avoidance, which is often difficult to overcome.

Yet, when the church functions as God intends, nothing else on earth works quite like it. Christ's bride is not an organization, but rather an organism. It's not so much about the hype of programs, but the health of people. She's not a building, but a body. When submitted to God and serving together in true community, the church is a family that will surround people with strength and grace, while continually pointing toward the abundant life in Christ.

In the body of Christ, you will grow faster in your walk with God.

Certainly we can grow spiritually on our own, but when we join in and get in step with a body of believers, it can accelerate our growth through accountability and synergy.

Accountability simply means everyone in the group has each other's back, and everyone is encouraged to grow and mature. This communal expectation assumes you will grow. You've joined a team with a clear goal and motivation for each individual member's success.

Synergy means the cohesion of the group is a greater force than the individual sum of its members. Together, they produce an overall stronger result than if each person works alone toward the same goal. As the writer of Ecclesiastes teaches:

> Two are better than one,
>> because they have a good return for their labor:
> If either of them falls down,
>> one can help the other up.
> But pity anyone who falls
>> and has no one to help them up (Ecclesiastes 4:9–10).

The Calgary Stampede has been known for many years as one of the premier rodeos in the world. One of their most exciting and anticipated events is the Heavy Horse Pull. The story is told of the year when a horse pulled 9,000 pounds, while another pulled 8,000 pounds. At the end of the event, the owners of the top two horses decided to see what both animals could do working together. Teamed up, you'd expect them to pull 17,000 pounds, right? Wrong. When harnessed together, they pulled 30,000 pounds!

The law of synergism caused the combined action of the two horses to be greater than the sum of their efforts working alone. Oddly enough, it's like saying 1 + 1 = 3. But, more accurately, it's more about multiplication than addition. Much more can be done through team effort than can be accomplished solo. And this truth leads perfectly into our next point.

In the body of Christ, you become a part of a movement larger than yourself.

Studies of the Millennial Generation — those whose birth years range from 1980 to 2000 — reveal the importance and power of relationships. While these people represent the least religious generation in American history, they also deeply value service to others by working together. What at first glance seems to be bad news for the church may actually turn into a powerful motivator for involvement in ministry. Thankfully, God knows exactly the dynamics of each generation and also what it takes to engage them in his kingdom.[19]

If we wake up every morning focused on ourselves and wondering why the world isn't making us happy, this approach to life isn't going to be satisfying and fulfilling in the long term. But when we engage in the church and see ourselves as a part of a far larger plan and purpose, we are infused with the power of eternity. We can indeed accomplish those "greater things" Christ referred to.

In closing, what does God use as the primary vehicle to get his "Upper Story" intertwined with our "Lower Story"? The church.

So, to think like Jesus, you must ask yourself this question: "Do I believe I have a role and responsibility in the church for God to use me in accomplishing his purposes today?"

Humanity

> For God so loved the world that he gave his
> only Son, that whoever believes in him shall not
> perish but have eternal life.
>
> JOHN 3:16

It's easy to become both overwhelmed and desensitized as we listen to the daily news reports. The massive problems throughout the world — poverty, disease, natural disasters, economic crises, random violence, sadistic dictators, nuclear threats — make it seem as though some kind of evil is destined for each day's headlines.

Yet, the focus for us really isn't on saving the world, but rather first on loving and obeying Jesus. The central question is not, "What problem of the world do I attempt to solve?" but rather "What would Jesus have me do for him?" Not only is the focus vastly different, but the motivation comes from the proper place. As Jesus said, we are to love the Lord, and then our neighbors as ourselves.

Simply deciding to be humanitarian is certainly a noble goal. But while social justice has become an increasing focus of the church in the past decade, obeying God and joining him in his work are the best labors of love we can offer as we serve the One who saved us. Jesus himself is our goal and purpose; the work is simply the result of what we do as we walk with him inside a relationship.

The apostle Paul shared the motivation for his tireless work in spreading the gospel to as many as possible:

He is the one we proclaim, admonishing and teaching every-one with all wisdom, so that we may present everyone fully mature in Christ. To this end I strenuously contend with all the energy Christ so powerfully works in me (Colossians 1:28–29).

KEY QUESTION: How does God see people— the masses of humanity?

We've already looked at John 3:16 in relation to God's love for us, but let's take a fresh look at this passage from a different version of the Bible through the filter of mankind's need for salvation.

"This is how much God loved the world: He gave his Son, his one and only Son. And this is why: so that no one need be destroyed; by believing in him, anyone can have a whole and last-ing life. God didn't go to all the trouble of sending his Son merely to point an accusing finger, telling the world how bad it was. He came to help, to put the world right again" (John 3:16–18 MSG).

Scripture is clear to communicate that God loves all people the same. His heart is to take us back to the garden. He loves the man in prison who committed heinous crimes as much as he does the faithful Sunday school teacher. He loves the tiny child struggling to survive in the desert of the Sudan as much as the Hollywood celebrity living in luxury. God sees all; he hears all; he loves all.

As the apostle Paul worked diligently to establish and sustain churches, his calling from God was always crystal clear, as is ours — to reach out to *all* people:

I am obligated both to Greeks and non-Greeks, both to the wise and the foolish. That is why I am so eager to preach the gospel also to you who are in Rome.

For I am not ashamed of the gospel, because it is the power of God that brings salvation to everyone who believes: first to the Jew, then to the Gentile. For in the gospel the righteousness of God is revealed—a righteousness that is by faith from first to last, just as it is written: "The righteous will live by faith."

The wrath of God is being revealed from heaven against all the godlessness and wickedness of people, who suppress the truth by their wickedness, since what may be known about God is plain to them, because God has made it plain to them. For since the creation of the world God's invisible qualities—his eternal power and divine nature—have been clearly seen, being understood from what has been made, so that people are without excuse (Romans 1:14–20).

Since "the wrath of God is being revealed from heaven against all the godlessness and wickedness of people," this is exactly why *all* people need to be saved. As the old adage goes, "The ground is level at the foot of the cross." Note also this phrase in verse 20: "people are without excuse." God says he will reveal himself in some manner to everyone. An invitation to salvation is offered to mankind.

All have sinned.

All wickedness must be punished.

All need salvation.

All are offered salvation.

All are without excuse.

KEY IDEA: I believe all people are loved by God and need Jesus Christ as their Savior.

We have established that God loves all people and desires to save everyone. So, why do we need Jesus?

The wrath of God has been satisfied through Christ's sacrifice on the cross. John records these words of Jesus: "I am the way and the truth and the life. No one comes to the Father except through me" (John 14:6).

This continues the pattern of all-inclusive language. "No one" comes to God except through Jesus. He has provided the way; therefore, all can be saved through him. Many have been offended these days with Christians' believing there is only one way to God, when in reality there should be great celebration that a way has been provided at all!

KEY APPLICATION: What difference does this make in the way I live?

How would life change if we started to see people as God sees them? How would the world change if you and I truly believed the only way for people to enter heaven is through Christ?

We value all human life.

From the womb to the tomb, we place high value on human life. Each person is formed and knit together by God in the womb of their mother (see Psalm 139:13). The oldest person in the world has not diminished in value one ounce in God's eyes or in ours.

We see and treat all people the way God sees and treats them.

In the gospel of Luke, we read about what happened one night when Jesus was having dinner at the home of a prominent Pharisee, a Jewish religious leader:

> When he [Jesus] noticed how the guests picked the places of honor at the table, he told them this parable: "When someone invites you to a wedding feast, do not take the place of honor, for a person more distinguished than you may have been invited. If so, the host who invited both of you will come and say to you, 'Give this person your seat.' Then, humiliated, you will have to take the least important place. But when you are invited, take the lowest place, so that when your host comes, he will say to you, 'Friend, move up to a better place.' Then you will be honored in the presence of all the other guests. For all those who exalt themselves will be humbled, and those who humble themselves will be exalted" (Luke 14:7–11).

Jesus is really speaking tongue in cheek to them. He thinks this system of placing human value on people is totally inconsistent with God's design. He gets at the heart of the matter with his next words to the prominent Pharisee:

> Then Jesus said to his host, "When you give a luncheon or dinner, do not invite your friends, your brothers or sisters, your relatives, or your rich neighbors; if you do, they may invite you back and so you will be repaid. But when you give a banquet, invite the poor, the crippled, the lame, the blind, and you will be blessed. Although they cannot repay you, you will be repaid at the resurrection of the righteous" (Luke 14:12–14).

God looks into our hearts and watches over our invitation list. When we show equal value to broken, bruised, and abandoned people in our society, God takes note and promises to reward us for such Godlike behavior. Authentic behavior flows from a heart of genuine belief in human value.

What made Christ's vision for the church so unique was the mixed group of people who assembled at the table for fellowship and a meal at the church service.

> In Christ Jesus you are all children of God through faith, for all of you who were baptized into Christ have clothed yourselves with Christ. There is neither Jew nor Gentile, neither slave nor free, nor is there male and female, for you are all one in Christ Jesus. If you belong to Christ, then you are Abraham's seed, and heirs according to the promise (Galatians 3:26–29).

We are compelled to tell all people about Jesus.

Having been a pastor for the past several years in the Hill Country of Texas, I think it's fitting to share the story of "Choctaw" Bill Robinson, an ordained circuit-riding preacher in the mid-1800s in the Lone Star State. He started at least twenty congregations throughout his ministry. But the unique aspect of Robinson's ministry, which earned him his nickname, was his faithfulness to preach the gospel to both the white man and the Native American. He showed no favoritism or discrimination toward either. He was responsible for converting new settlers to Christ, as well as small tribes of Native Americans. "Choctaw" Bill saw all the population of the vast territory of Texas as needing the gospel of Christ.[20]

We can become excited about telling people about a new job, a new baby, a new home, or a new car. While these are all worthwhile experiences, as Christians, we hold the greatest news of all time in our hearts. I don't intend at all to heap guilt or to put a burden on anyone, but rather to try to inspire us to see how we can revolutionize the lives of people, while fulfilling our ultimate purpose in being children of God.

The apostle Peter exhorts, "In your hearts revere Christ as Lord. Always be prepared to give an answer to everyone who asks you to give the reason for the hope that you have" (1 Peter 3:15).

When should we be prepared? Always.

What should we give them? An answer.

Who should we be prepared to give an answer to? Everyone.

What is the reason for our hope and our answer? Christ, who is Lord of all.

By sharing the gospel with all people, wherever we go, we have the opportunity to ...

- change the world by changing people's hearts
- change family legacies, as well as generations
- become more loving people, as we learn to value all

If God has his way in our minds and hearts through our obedience, we can accomplish these things, but it will require us to reach out. As Paul writes:

> How, then, can they call on the one they have not believed in? And how can they believe in the one of whom they have not heard? And how can they hear without someone preaching to them? And how can anyone preach unless they are sent? As it

is written: "How beautiful are the feet of those who bring good news!" (Romans 10:14–15).

There is someone right now in your circle of influence who needs to hear your story of salvation and redemption. God has placed people in your life, and he will bless you with the privilege of seeing them come into his kingdom. Imagine one day a person sharing his or her life story and, at a crucial point, the person says, "And then there was someone who cared enough to share Jesus with me." Such a testimony, my friend, is the abundant life at its finest moment!

Do you believe God loves all people? Do you see all people the way God sees them? Do you believe God has made salvation through Christ available for all people? If you do, you will be compelled to show respect to all people and love them enough to tell them about Jesus. If we refuse to show respect and love, you and I must face the hard fact that we don't see people the way God sees them. For me, I know I have more pondering to do about the depth of my belief. How about you?

Compassion

Defend the weak and the fatherless;
uphold the cause of the poor and the oppressed.
Rescue the weak and the needy;
deliver them from the hand of the wicked.

PSALM 82:3–4

"Am I my brother's keeper?" We all know this question well. Cain's words in Genesis 4:9 have been used and misused countless times. Jesus' teaching, as well as his actions throughout his life, answered this question with a clear "Yes!" for all who follow him. We *are* our brother's — and sister's — keeper. In fact, a spirit of caring for others permeates the entire New Testament.

KEY QUESTION: What is my responsibility to other people?

If anyone responds to the first two "Thinking Like Jesus" beliefs of *God* and *Personal God* with, "I do not believe there is a God, and I do not believe in a personal god," then hedonism — the philosophy of "let us eat and drink, for tomorrow we die" (as Paul quotes it in 1 Corinthians 15:32) — actually makes a lot of sense. If someone truly believes this life is all there is, why would they want to care about someone else? Why waste precious time trying to meet someone else's needs if this life is all there is? In this belief system, self-focus not only makes sense; it is quite a logical way to live.

But as followers of Jesus, what if we adopt the opposite end of the spectrum as our driving force in life — becoming like Christ for the sake of others? What if love for people went from a beautiful chorus we chant in church to a mission statement we live out in life?

> Suppose a brother or a sister is without clothes and daily food. If one of you says to them, "Go in peace; keep warm and well fed," but does nothing about their physical needs, what good is it? (James 2:15–16).

> As God's chosen people, holy and dearly loved, clothe yourselves with compassion, kindness, humility, gentleness and patience (Colossians 3:12).

> All of you, be like-minded, be sympathetic, love one another, be compassionate and humble (1 Peter 3:8).

To whom are we to be compassionate, kind, humble, gentle, patient, sympathetic, and loving? Everyone else on the planet — our neighbors.

KEY IDEA: I believe God calls all Christians to show compassion to people in need.

Jesus makes it clear we are to follow him down the path of compassion:

> "Even the Son of Man did not come to be served, but to serve, and to give his life as a ransom for many" (Mark 10:45).

> "Greater love has no one than this: to lay down one's life for one's friends. You are my friends if you do what I command. I no longer call you servants, because a servant does not know his master's business. Instead, I have called you friends, for everything that I learned from my Father I have made known to you. You did not choose me, but I chose you and appointed you so that you might go and bear fruit—fruit that will last—and so that whatever you ask in my name the Father will give you" (John 15:13–16).

Jesus has brought us into the family business — placing others first to meet needs today, while also changing the future for anyone who will respond to the message of salvation. Those who are his friends will be willing to serve as he did. In God's kingdom, even helping a person with a temporary necessity has an eternal purpose.

In Matthew 25:34 – 40, Jesus teaches his followers the divine priority of serving people. We see clearly the degree to which Jesus pays attention to the details of our lives — and he calls us to this same awareness in serving others:

> "Then the King will say to those on his right, 'Come, you who are blessed by my Father; take your inheritance, the kingdom prepared for you since the creation of the world. For I was hungry and you gave me something to eat, I was thirsty and you gave me something to drink, I was a stranger and you invited me in, I needed clothes and you clothed me, I was sick and you looked after me, I was in prison and you came to visit me.'
>
> "Then the righteous will answer him, 'Lord, when did we see you hungry and feed you, or thirsty and give you something to drink? When did we see you a stranger and invite you in, or needing clothes and clothe you? When did we see you sick or in prison and go to visit you?'
>
> "The King will reply, 'Truly I tell you, whatever you did for one of the least of these brothers and sisters of mine, you did for me.' "

Jesus made our mission abundantly clear in meeting the needs of the forgotten, unlovely, and unpopular — "the least of these." His declaration that to serve them is to serve him is both counter-cultural and life-changing.

KEY APPLICATION: What difference does this make in the way I live?

If we choose to show compassion to people as God does, then ...

- we will change our priorities and how we use our time
- we are set free to give, because we trust God for our needs
- people who have been forgotten by society will be cared for and restored
- we will truly reach our neighborhoods and our cities
- the Spirit of Christ will be alive and well in our lives

The oft-quoted phrase "people don't care how much you know until they know how much you care" will come to life. As people see how much we care and ask us what we know, we may respond with, "It's not *what* we know, but *who* we know. His name is Jesus, and he would love to meet you."

In 1952, evangelist Everett Swanson went to South Korea to preach the gospel to troops in the Republic of Korea's army. During his visit, he was deeply moved by the number of children orphaned by the war. He discussed this issue with a missionary, who challenged Rev. Swanson, "You have seen the tremendous needs and unparalleled opportunities of this land. What do you intend to do about it?"

In effect, this missionary was saying, "Are you going to just feel sympathy for these children, or are you going to express compassion?"

Swanson returned to the United States and, along with his wife, Miriam, and with the help of Dr. Gus and Helen Hemwall, a ministry was launched on behalf of these orphans. At his revival meetings, Rev. Swanson began to share about the needs of the Korean children. Christians began to donate funds to help meet daily living needs. By 1954, the sponsorship program still offered today was born, whereby people could give a monthly gift to help provide food, shelter, medical care, and Bible instruction for a specific child.

In 1963, Swanson was becoming uneasy about his name being the focus of this growing ministry. He was inspired by Jesus' words in Matthew 15:32: "I have compassion for these people ... I do not want to send them away hungry." So the ministry name was changed and is now known worldwide as Compassion International. What began as a missionary's challenge to an evangelist who saw a need is today a vital ministry that serves more than one million children in more than twenty-five nations.

While compassion is a deeply emotive feeling any human may experience, the Christian belief of compassion is coupled with the motivation to act on those feelings. The divine filter of seeing people as God sees them will lead us to both see the need and find the resources to meet them. So let me offer a simple assignment: the next time you feel compassion welling up in your soul, let it trigger action in your hands and feet to be Jesus to "the least of these."

Stewardship

> The earth is the LORD's, and everything in it,
> the world, and all who live in it;
> for he founded it on the seas
> and established it on the waters.
>
> PSALM 24:1–2

Typically when we talk about the word *stewardship* in the church, we immediately connect it to putting money in an offering plate — causing our minds to go quickly to our wallets and purses. We think about handing over money, and both the definition and connotation quickly become narrow and negative for many.

While giving money to the church, including the idea of tithing — giving 10 percent — certainly is an aspect of stewardship, by no means does it capture the entire concept. To fully comprehend the biblical belief of stewardship, we have to think much bigger and broader.

KEY QUESTION: How much does God want of me?

The bottom line is that God wants all you have. The answer to this key question is this: 100 percent. And by the way, for the Christian, this is nonnegotiable.

So we now want to know, "Why would God want all of me? Why does he want *all* I have?"

The simple and obvious answer is that everything is already his anyway. But the deeper and more personal answer is because this is the best opportunity for us, as well as for those around us.

Remember the miser from the "Think Like Jesus" section in the introduction? His greed hurt him, his relationship with his friend, and his reputation. Giving all we have to God not only offers freedom to our souls and blesses our lives, but blesses all those we encounter in our circles of influence as well.

The only passage of Scripture in which God invites us to test him is Malachi 3:10 – 12:

> "Bring the whole tithe into the storehouse, that there may be food in my house. Test me in this," says the LORD Almighty, "and see if I will not throw open the floodgates of heaven and pour out so much blessing that there will not be room enough to store it. I will prevent pests from devouring your crops, and the vines in your fields will not drop their fruit before it is ripe," says the LORD Almighty. "Then all the nations will call you blessed, for yours will be a delightful land," says the LORD Almighty.

This passage is full of personal language from God, offering powerful promises of blessing for those who obediently give to the Lord. He shows us what he is able to do in the life of a faithful steward.

Jesus taught frequently about this spiritual dynamic, including these words in his sermon on the plateau as recorded in Luke 6:38:

> "Give, and it will be given to you. A good measure, pressed down, shaken together and running over, will be poured into your lap. For with the measure you use, it will be measured to you."

As we can see, God is serious about this matter, so let's introduce our key idea.

KEY IDEA: I believe everything I am and everything I own belong to God.

If we agree that 100 percent of all we own comes from God, then a begrudging attitude toward him in sharing all he gives will smack of the miser. The apostle Paul writes in 2 Corinthians 9:6 – 8:

Remember this: Whoever sows sparingly will also reap sparingly, and whoever sows generously will also reap generously. Each of you should give what you have decided in your heart to give, not reluctantly or under compulsion, for God loves a cheerful giver. And God is able to bless you abundantly, so that in all things at all times, having all that you need, you will abound in every good work.

There are two important points about this passage with regard to stewardship. First, Paul's teaching parallels God's challenge in Malachi. Sow sparingly, and you reap sparingly. Sow generously, and you reap generously. If you give generously, God can bless abundantly. Second, the decision of what we should give is made in the heart — the catalyst for our actions.

In his sermon recorded by Matthew, Jesus said, "For where your treasure is, there your heart will be also" (Matthew 6:21). Interestingly, the converse of this Scripture is true as well: Where your heart is, there your treasure will be also.

Let's expand now to the true definition and big picture of stewardship.

The biblical idea is that through a relationship with God, we move from the title of owner to the position of manager. A steward is simply a manager. We deed over to God ownership of all things in our lives — external and internal — and we then take on the management of all he gives. This means not only the physical — money, house, cars, resources — but also our gifts, talents, personality, and intellect. I am all his. You are all his. All we are and all we own belong to God. He now decides what we receive, what we do with what we have, and what we give.

One of the growing trends in business over the past twenty years is this scenario: A corporation takes notice of a smaller company that has a similar business and decides that this smaller company might benefit the larger firm. The corporation approaches the company owner and says, "We want to buy your business, take over your debt, offer you our resources, and hire you and your staff to run it for us, but you'll now belong to us." For the small business owner, the thought of shifting the constant strain of dealing with finances to someone else and concentrating on the work at hand is attractive. This method of growth for large companies has become commonplace. Obviously, there are a multitude of challenges in making these ventures work, but many succeed quite well, and when they do, everyone wins.

This is exactly the concept of stewardship in a modern-day example. You "own" your own life, but your "business" is quite dysfunctional and deeply in debt. Christ comes to you and says, "I'm offering to buy you out. Redeem your life. Pay off all your debt that you could never repay. I will give you all of my resources, and you can then manage what I give you." In this transaction, what do you "owe" him in return? As stewards, we give back our lives and resources for others' good and his glory. Love him; love neighbor — with all we are and all we have.

KEY APPLICATION: What difference does this make in the way I live?

We move from owner to manager.

My central question now becomes, "What does God want me to do with all the resources he has put into my care?"

We approach every day as a living sacrifice to God.

Romans 12:1 provides an explicit answer to this question of what God wants us to do with what he has given us:

> *I urge you, brothers and sisters, in view of God's mercy, to offer your bodies as a living sacrifice, holy and pleasing to God— this is your true and proper worship.*

At first read, this verse may be a bit confusing. After all, isn't a "living sacrifice" an oxymoron? A sacrifice is a living thing *killed* as a substitution for another. Once a sacrifice is made, how can it then keep on living?

Here's how: The only way is for the sacrifice to actually live on the altar 24/7 — staying alive, yet always prepared to die. Ever-present in the state of offering, but continuing to live and serve as the sacrifice. So we place ourselves on God's altar and live there in "view of God's mercy." Christ's own sacrifice for us is the only way this is made possible. As we stated earlier, we stay off the throne of our lives, where God belongs, and live on the altar, where we belong. And by our remaining a living sacrifice, we will be the proper stewards of all God gives.

If we truly believed that all we are and all we have belong to God, then in our lifetime we might make the same difference in our day as the early church made in theirs. With dividing lines erased and walls torn down by such sacrifice, we would be free to share and give — and see dramatic changes in our world and in the lives of those we serve.

The closing questions are these: "Have I deeded my life to God and then accepted stewardship of all he has given me? Am I 100 percent his?"

Eternity

"Do not let your hearts be troubled. You believe in God; believe also in me. My Father's house has many rooms; if that were not so, would I have told you that I am going there to prepare a place for you?"

JOHN 14:1–2

In light of Christ's forgiveness of us and his provision of all his resources and qualities to us in the present, what should we then believe about the days to come?

KEY QUESTION: What is going to happen in the future?

Blaise Pascal was an inventor, mathematician, physicist, and theological writer in the 1600s. In the mid-1650s, he wrote the *Pénsees*. Contained in this writing, which ironically wasn't formally published until after his death, was an apologetic argument that became known as "Pascal's Wager." The basis of this thought had to do with a human gamble regarding eternity.

"God is, or He is not." But to which side shall we incline? Reason can decide nothing here. There is an infinite chaos, which separated us. A game is being played at the extremity of this infinite distance where heads or tails will turn up ... Which will you choose then? Let us see. Since you must choose, let us see which interests you least. You have two things to lose, the true and the good; and two things to stake, your reason and your will,

88

your knowledge and your happiness; and your nature has two things to shun, error and misery. Your reason is no more shocked in choosing one rather than the other, since you must of necessity choose ... But your happiness? Let us weigh the gain and the loss in wagering that God is ... If you gain, you gain all; if you lose, you lose nothing. Wager, then, without hesitation that He is.[21]

As science and theology collided in his heart, Pascal concluded that belief in a God who says he has provided life for eternity makes for a potentially happier life than not believing. The consequences for *not* believing far outweigh those for believing. He also states each person who lives must make this wager, which will affect how they live and what they decide.

The Christian is on the other side of this dilemma of the soul — now looking to build God's kingdom for the time spent in eternity, as well as preparing others for his return.

KEY IDEA: I believe there is a heaven and a hell and that Jesus will return to judge all people and to establish his eternal kingdom.

The central belief about our future and eternity is that when we die, our bodies return to the earth, but our spirits live on. Those spirits go to one of two places — heaven or hell.

Even though I'm a pastor, I honestly don't like the part about hell. I never have, and I never will. My job, and even the way others perceive us pastors, would be easier if it were not a part of the gospel message. But as we previously discussed about the Bible, we have to take God's truth as a total work and even accept the areas we don't like or wish were not there. Of course, those who have received Christ's offer of salvation by grace no longer need to be concerned about this matter anyway, because he has removed this fear from our future.

Let me emphasize an important point here: When we die and go into eternity, this moment is not the end, as many tend to believe.

Jesus Christ is going to return to the earth, and his first order of business will be to judge mankind. When Jesus returns, he'll make all things right, and everything will come under the authority of his justice. He will throw Satan and his followers, along with sin and death, into the lake of fire. Christ's followers will then receive an imperishable, resurrected body, just as Christ now has. Jesus and his people will then reside on a new earth surrounded by a new heaven. For the Christian, this is the future. When we say, "The best is yet to come," we can confidently mean what we say!

On this great day, God himself will live among us and the original garden of three will expand into a great city of millions.

> The LORD reigns, he is robed in majesty;
>   the LORD is robed in majesty and armed with strength;
>   indeed, the world is established, firm and secure.
> Your throne was established long ago;
>   you are from all eternity (Psalm 93:1 – 2).

> Then I looked and heard the voice of many angels, numbering thousands upon thousands, and ten thousand times ten thousand. They encircled the throne and the living creatures and the elders. In a loud voice they were saying:

> "Worthy is the Lamb, who was slain,
>   to receive power and wealth and wisdom and strength
>   and honor and glory and praise!"

> Then I heard every creature in heaven and on earth and under the earth and on the sea, and all that is in them, saying:

> "To him who sits on the throne and to the Lamb
>   be praise and honor and glory and power,
>   for ever and ever!" (Revelation 5:11 – 13).

KEY APPLICATION: What difference does this make in the way I live?

If we truly believe God has prepared an eternal home for us — a house with many rooms, as Jesus explained in John 14 — then we can and will ...

- live with hope every day, regardless of the circumstances around us; life may or may not get better here, but we can know that God's home awaits us

- love people with freedom and boldness, because our future is secure in him

- lead more people into a relationship with Christ, because we want to share this great hope with others

I ask you to prayerfully take a moment to do an inventory of your relationships. How many non-Christians are currently in your circle of influence? And of these non-Christians in your circle, how many are you actively sharing God's love with? On the lines below, write their names. If you need more space, write in the margins.

_____

_____

_____

_____

_____

_____

_____

_____

_____

It is important to express here that, even if you cannot write down a name, this exercise is not intended to create any condemnation or blame. But the absence of a name should produce conviction in a Christ follower's life. If you have none, or maybe just one, then the motivation here is to gain a hunger and a drive to see others come to faith in Christ. There is no condemnation for what has *not* happened, but conviction toward obedience to see what *can* happen. If you have no names, don't wallow and waste any more time; simply rise up and get on a mission.

If, however, you wrote down several names, be encouraged that God is working on your behalf to use your every word and action to bring these people to him. Keep praying, be inspired, and never give up. Imagine one day each person giving a testimony of how you introduced him or her to freedom into eternity. Also, know you are simply a part of the salvation process in these lives, and God will most definitely use you as you submit to and serve him.

Paul described well to the church in Corinth his partnership approach of working with Apollos to reach people, while the work of salvation is up to God, the Gardener.

> What, after all, is Apollos? And what is Paul? Only servants, through whom you came to believe—as the Lord has assigned to each his task. I planted the seed, Apollos watered it, but God has been making it grow. So neither the one who plants nor the one who waters is anything, but only God, who makes things grow (1 Corinthians 3:5–7).

Let's give Jesus' brother, Jude, the last word as we wait for Jesus to return:

> You, dear friends, by building yourselves up in your most holy faith and praying in the Holy Spirit, keep yourselves in God's love as you wait for the mercy of our Lord Jesus Christ to bring you to eternal life (Jude 20–21).

PART 2

Act Like Jesus
What Should I Do?

Do you not know that in a race all the runners run,
but only one gets the prize? Run in such a way as to
get the prize. Everyone who competes in the games
goes into strict training. They do it to get a crown
that will not last, but we do it to get a crown that
will last forever. Therefore I do not run like someone
running aimlessly; I do not fight like a boxer beating
the air. No, I strike a blow to my body and make it my
slave so that after I have preached to others, I myself
will not be disqualified for the prize.

1 CORINTHIANS 9:24–27

The key beliefs covered in the last section drive the outcome of who we become. However, there is a difference between believing something as the right answer and believing something as a way of life. The first resides in the head alone; the latter camps out in the head *and* the heart. Growth begins by understanding spiritual beliefs in our mind but it cannot stop there. We must embrace these axioms and truths in our heart. When these beliefs take up residence in our heart, they will help form who we become. Why? Because we live from our heart.

So how do we transport biblical beliefs twelve inches from the head to the heart — from thinking to actions? The primary means is through engaging in *biblical practices*. In the epigraph at the beginning of page 93, Paul views these practices as spiritual disciplines. As a believer engages in them routinely and consistently, transformation occurs day by day. Spiritual muscles form. Spiritual lungs expand. The spiritual heart pumps stronger.

We cannot bring about inner transformation on our own. The living presence of the Spirit in our spirit (heart, will) empowers us as we yield to his influence and coaching in our lives. Because he resides in our spirit, he bypasses all the layers of complexity, where excuses and rationalizations creep in, and speaks directly to our heart. As we see in the illustration above, the presence of God moves us toward action. Right beliefs in the mind become outward expressions from the heart.

Jesus used the analogy of a vine in John 15 to explain this inner transformational process. When we accept and receive Christ into our lives, we are reconciled to God. Jesus said our "branches" (our very lives) are grafted into the vine of Christ. As we obey the commands of Jesus (practice the Christian life), the rich nutrients from the root of Christ are transferred into our branches. Eventually, rich, plump, tasty grapes appear on the end of our branches — the fruit of the Spirit.

As you turn the page you will be introduced to the top ten key practices of the Christian life. Together they answer the question, "What should I do?" Each chapter will address three areas:

1. **KEY QUESTION:** What life question does this practice answer?

2. **KEY IDEA:** What are the essentials of engaging in this spiritual practice?

3. **KEY APPLICATION:** What difference does this make in the way I live?

Spiritual exercising can be as challenging as physical exercising, but the outcome is undeniably beneficial. Spiritual fitness coach Paul offered this inspirational word to pump up young Timothy:

> *Physical training is of some value, but godliness has value for all things, holding promise for both the present life and the life to come. This is a trustworthy saying that deserves full acceptance (1 Timothy 4:8–9).*

As you learn about these amazingly life-giving spiritual disciplines, embrace them in your heart and make it your goal to strap on your spiritual tennis shoes and give them a try.

Worship

Come, let us sing for joy to the LORD;
  let us shout aloud to the Rock of our salvation.
Let us come before him with thanksgiving
  and extol him with music and song.

PSALM 95:1–2

Our simple definition for the practice of worship is "attributing worth to someone or something."

Worship is not an earthly event we attend, but rather a heavenly activity in which we take part. As Christians, in our personal and corporate worship of the one true God, we are attributing or ascribing worth to him, and to him alone. Regardless of the method of praise, whether singing, speaking, or any physical expression, we are both believing of him and communicating to him, "God, you are worthy." We are declaring that he is worthy — and everything and anything else is not.

KEY QUESTION: How do I honor God in the way he deserves?

When we worship God for who he is, we are simultaneously expressing these convictions:

1. We believe in the Trinity and declare he is the one true God
   (BELIEF: God)

2. We believe God is involved in and cares about our daily lives
   (BELIEF: Personal God)

3. We believe God has provided a way for us to be made right with him by his grace (BELIEF: Salvation)

4. We agree that God's Word directs our beliefs and actions (BELIEF: The Bible)

5. We believe we have significance because of the position and worth God has given us (BELIEF: Identity in Christ)

6. We recognize God as the head of the church (BELIEF: Church)

7. We believe our God loves all people (BELIEF: Humanity)

8. We desire to provide compassion to those in need because of who God is (BELIEF: Compassion)

9. We believe God is the owner of all things, including us (BELIEF: Stewardship)

10. We believe God has provided a way for us to live with him forever (BELIEF: Eternity)

As you can clearly see through these connections, there is a deep intertwining of the key beliefs with the practice of worship. Worship is the first spiritual discipline of a Christ follower that helps the key beliefs move from our head to our heart.

KEY IDEA: I worship God for who he is and what he has done for me.

In Jesus' encounter with a woman from Samaria as she drew water from a well, the conversation went to the subject of worship:

> *"Sir," the woman said, "I can see that you are a prophet. Our ancestors worshiped on this mountain, but you Jews claim that the place where we must worship is in Jerusalem."*
>
> *"Woman," Jesus replied, "believe me, a time is coming when you will worship the Father neither on this mountain nor in Jerusalem. You Samaritans worship what you do not know; we worship what we do know, for salvation is from the Jews. Yet a time is coming and has now come when the true worshipers will worship*

PRACTICE 1: Worship | 99

the Father in the Spirit and in truth, for they are the kind of worshipers the Father seeks. God is spirit, and his worshipers must worship in the Spirit and in truth. (John 4:19–24).

Jesus is stating that true worship is not about being at a precise geographic location, but rather about having an intimate spiritual longing. God seeks worshipers who, through the power of his Spirit, will attribute worth to him in any location and for the right reasons — because he is truth.

The psalms refer often to our worship of God for who he is and what he has done:

> *Ascribe to the LORD the glory due his name;*
>   *worship the LORD in the splendor of his holiness*
>   *(Psalm 29:2).*

> *Come, let us bow down in worship,*
>   *let us kneel before the LORD our Maker;*
> *for he is our God*
>   *and we are the people of his pasture,*
>   *the flock under his care (Psalm 95:6–7).*

> *With my mouth I will greatly extol the LORD;*
>   *in the great throng of worshipers I will praise him*
>   *(Psalm 109:30).*

While worship is a deeply personal matter, the practice is an ongoing activity of the church. If you've ever stood among a group of sold-out saints lifting up song together, you know how powerfully individual hearts can unite and work together to create a cathedral anywhere!

KEY APPLICATION: What difference does this make in the way I live?

- We daily acknowledge God for who he is and what he has done for us.

- We worship God, privately and corporately, with the songs we sing, the words we speak, and the way we live our lives.

- When we attribute worth to God as a child of God, unmerited worth is attributed to us.

Since the fall of mankind in the garden of Eden, our greatest struggle is wanting to be our own god. While most of us would not wish to have the responsibility and burden of calling the shots for the entire world, we *do* want to be the god of our own lives — to do what we want, when we want, where we want, with whom we want.

Therefore, when we engage in the practice of worship, we crawl off *the throne* of God, where we do not belong, and crawl onto *the altar* of God, where we do belong. The quite amazing exchange when we surrender control and attribute worth to God is that he, in turn, attributes his worth back to us as his children. Worship expresses the relationship we have with God — and the stronger the relationship and the deeper the intimacy, the greater the worship. This then causes a deeper love for God.

I don't know about you, but I would rather rest in the fact that I am a child of God than wear myself out trying to be god. I much prefer to receive the *blessing* he does intend for me rather than to bear the *burden* he never intended for me.

To better illustrate and understand this connection of worship in the heart of a believer, let's look at a passage involving David when he was king over Israel.

In 2 Samuel 6, we read the story of how David visits Obed-Edom's house to retrieve the ark, which he and his men successfully return to Jerusalem through proper transport and sacrifice — this time obeying the Lord's instructions in detail.

As David comes into the city in the presence of all the people, he is filled with gratitude to God to have the ark in its rightful place. He proceeds to strip off his kingly clothes, right down to a linen ephod — an undergarment commonly worn by the men who assisted the priests in religious exercises. Even in David's choice of apparel, he was humbling himself before God, while expressing great praise to God through his outward actions. The author of 2 Samuel writes:

> Wearing a linen ephod, David was dancing before the LORD with all his might, while he and all Israel were bringing up the ark of the LORD with shouts and the sound of trumpets.
>
> As the ark of the LORD was entering the City of David, Michal daughter of Saul watched from a window. And when she saw King David leaping and dancing before the LORD, she despised him in her heart.
>
> They brought the ark of the LORD and set it in its place inside the tent that David had pitched for it, and David sacrificed burnt offerings and fellowship offerings before the LORD (2 Samuel 6:14–17).

David's deep respect, awe, joy, gratitude, and relief at God's blessings overwhelmed him to the point where he didn't care about anyone or anything — except worshiping God in the Spirit and in truth.

Michal, Saul's daughter, was embarrassed by David's actions and cared more about whether others would be offended than about the authority of God. While David exuded abandonment to the Lord, Michal exhibited the pride of life.

Could Michal have looked out the window, seen the ark, and become so excited about the returning presence of God that she would hurry down and join in the celebration with David? Certainly. We see how Miriam responded in worship with Moses on the other side of the parted sea; Michal had a choice in her response as well.

Now, the point here is not about what we wear or about whether or not we leap and dance. The heart of this passage is about the heart of the person! Both David and Michal witnessed the ark — the symbol of God's presence — coming into Jerusalem. Both responded according to what lay in their souls. Therein is the true practice of worship—our hearts surrendered and then submitted to God, attributing all we are and all we have to him.

With many denominational lines drawn today over expressions of worship, we often place too much focus, and at times even judgment, on how much or how little someone outwardly displays their praise. We must first understand that worship is about how much love and devotion exist in our minds and hearts for God. Someone in quiet meditation can be just as deep in adoration of God as one whose hands are lifted and voice is singing—and vice versa.

True worship is simply a reflection of the heart of a believer. In closing, consider these questions.

- To whom or what do you attribute the *most* worth in your own life?

- Is the location of your worship confined to a geographic place, or is your worship freely displayed, in the power of his Spirit and in accordance with truth, anywhere?

- Do you relate more to David or to Michal?

When we stand in the presence of a holy God, as David did and as Jesus invited the woman at the well to do, our hearts will be quick to give him the authority and the honor he deserves. The growing practice of worship will then create an overarching hunger for greater depth in all the other practices.

Prayer

If I had cherished sin in my heart,
   the LORD would not have listened;
but God has surely listened
   and has heard my prayer.
Praise be to God,
   who has not rejected my prayer
   or withheld his love from me!
                              PSALM 66:18–20

The psalmist declares in no uncertain terms this truth: Prayer works. Whatever he had asked of God, he received an answer from the Lord — and he wanted everyone to know. Like a satisfied customer singing the praises of a revered product, he announces to the world that prayer produces real results.

When we engage in the action and discipline of prayer to know God better, we convey, as well as reinforce, our belief in *God*. For most of us, we are expressing the reality that he is not necessarily the God we want — we would actually prefer ourselves, as our sinful nature leads us to do — but have come to know he is the God we truly need. Whether it is someone's occasional 9-1-1 prayers or the believer's daily divine dialogue, there is always a distinct element of submission in every heartfelt prayer, whereby we are admitting we have a need we cannot possibly meet on our own.

When we cast our cares on God, lay our burdens before him, and share our hearts with him, we reinforce and express the truth that he is a *personal God*. We pray, believing and trusting he is involved in and cares about our daily lives.

When we ask God to give us direction for life, we are reinforcing and expressing the belief of *stewardship*. Because God is the owner of everything in our lives, we go to him for the next step in every walk of life.

Once again, the practices of Jesus connect to the beliefs of Jesus. In this practice, Christ calls us to pray as he prayed.

KEY QUESTION: How do I grow by communicating with God?

To learn how to act like Jesus in this area of prayer, we must look at the times in the Gospels when he prayed. Let's begin with his priority of prayer. Mark records this in the first chapter of his gospel: "Very early in the morning, while it was still dark, Jesus got up, left the house and went off to a solitary place, where he prayed" (Mark 1:35).

While this is a straightforward and simple verse, what can we learn here?

Prayer was a priority to Jesus. In this verse, we see he went away from everyone else to be alone. No distractions; no other voices; no one but the Father and him.

And then he prayed — sharing his heart with God and listening to him. We don't know how long or what he talked to his Father about, but dedicated time was set aside for communication with the Father before he went about his day.

It's important not to view these focused moments of prayer as our "God time," and then to make the rest of our day all about us. Rather, the focused time with God sets the tone for our day, starting an ongoing dialogue that will continue throughout the ups and downs of daily life.

If Jesus needed to spend time alone with the Father, talking to him and listening to him, how much more should we prioritize this practice!

KEY IDEA: **I pray to God to know him,
to find direction for my life,
and to lay my requests before him.**

All of John 17 contains one of Jesus' prayers. A remarkable aspect of this dialogue is that Jesus prays for everyone who will ever believe in him. Set aside time soon to read this chapter, so you can be instructed in how to pray and be encouraged by what Jesus asks the Father on our behalf.

In Matthew's gospel, Jesus warns his followers against praying "like the hypocrites," only practicing prayer as an outward display of religiousness for human approval (Matthew 6:5). Jesus makes himself clear about prayer by starting with simple words of instruction:

> *"This, then, is how you should pray:*
>
> *" 'Our Father in heaven,*
> *hallowed be your name,*
> *your kingdom come,*
> *your will be done,*
> *   on earth as it is in heaven.*
> *Give us today our daily bread.*
> *And forgive us our debts,*
> *   as we also have forgiven our debtors.*
> *And lead us not into temptation,*
> *   but deliver us from the evil one' "* (Matthew 6:9– 13).

Jesus' prayer was concise, yet detailed. He prayed for body and soul to be taken care of. He modeled how to ask for forgiveness and protection. He expressed praise of the Father and submission to him. Flowery, religious words are not necessary or required — just honest and open requests shared.

In Matthew, Mark, and Luke, we eavesdrop by the door of heaven and hear Jesus taking his greatest burden to God — the reality of the cross. Again, we see him go off alone, speak his mind, and yet fully submit. And we see God answer, not in the way Jesus might want, but in such a way that provision did come. This agonizing passage provides us with much to learn with regard to prayer:

> He withdrew about a stone's throw beyond them, knelt down and prayed, "Father, if you are willing, take this cup from me; yet not my will, but yours be done." An angel from heaven appeared to him and strengthened him (Luke 22:41–43).

We can be encouraged through this exchange that, while God will not always deliver us *from* our circumstances, he will deliver us *through* the circumstances, by giving us what we need in order to accomplish what he asks us to do.

KEY APPLICATION: What difference does this make in the way I live?

- We pray to align our lives with God's will and story.
- We pray to lay our burdens before God to find peace.
- We pray to avoid making any major decision without seeking God.
- We pray for others.

If there is any subject the psalmists consistently address, it is that of prayer. We see humility coupled with boldness, awe joined with confidence — not in oneself, but in God. The many Scriptures in the book of Psalms inspire and challenge us to go before God and to speak to him about the deep need in our lives. Note the power and emotion captured in the words. Here are just a few examples:

> I call on you, my God, for you will answer me;
> turn your ear to me and hear my prayer (Psalm 17:6).

> Hear my prayer, O God;
> listen to the words of my mouth (Psalm 54:2).

> Listen to my prayer, O God,
> do not ignore my plea (Psalm 55:1).

May my prayer come before you;
   turn your ear to my cry (Psalm 88:2).

I cry to you for help, LORD;
   in the morning my prayer comes before you
      (Psalm 88:13).

While the word *prayer* creates much religious connotation for some and intimidation for others, we must remember an amazing truth: we are being invited to speak with and listen to our Creator and Redeemer. He is not distant; he is listening. He does not keep us from going to him; he invites us to come to him.

One of the most remarkable verses in all of Scripture to show us the kind of relationship God wants with us through prayer is found in Moses' story: "The LORD would speak to Moses face to face, as one speaks to a friend" (Exodus 33:11).

Earlier, I shared the story of the birth of our son David, who was born without a left hand. Prayer was a key spiritual practice to not only help me process this difficult event in our lives but also to move the reality of my identity, and my son's identity, in Christ from my head to my heart.

During this time, I began by praying psalms of lament to the Lord: *Why, Lord, did you let this happen to me? I serve you as a pastor of a church — not perfectly, but wholeheartedly. Why could you not pass this burden on to someone who doesn't even believe in you? Have I done something wrong to deserve this?*

I never sensed God was angry with me for speaking to him with such honesty. Actually, I felt as though he were whispering to me, *Go ahead, I can handle this. I love you. Keep talking honestly to me, and we will get to the bottom of this. I will show you something I have wanted you to see for a long time.*

In many extended moments of silence, when I didn't know what else to say or how to pray, God began speaking back to me — not in an audible voice, but directly to my spirit. I felt a little like Job when God started speaking to him after Job had shared his best thoughts and emotions upon losing his wealth, health, and all of his children.

"Randy, my son, I have nothing in my being that seeks to harm you. The darkness and pain of the world are caused by sin, not by me. I have come to redeem the pain caused by sin. Randy, my son, I will use this situation to show you — and your son — who I really am. If you capture this, it will be more valuable than having three hands. Randy, my son, I have given your son everything he needs to be and do everything I am calling him to be and do. Randy, my son, it is time to shift your sense of worth from your performance to your position. You are my son. You do not have to perform to be a somebody; you already are a somebody in my eyes.

"Randy, my son, you need to teach this to your son. He will learn this from how you live, not by your words alone. You have four years before he realizes he is missing a hand. This gives you four years to learn to place your identity in your position as my son. Randy, my son, if you get this truth embedded into your heart, you will be free — free from the exhausting life of trying to gain and sustain status in the world. This is a great gift to give to all your children."

Prayer is a conversation with God. We lay our honest requests before God, our need for daily bread. Yet, we clarify, as Jesus did, that we want God's will to be done over our will, trusting his way to be good and right. As we rest in the presence of God, he will speak and show us his will in his perfect timing.

As I look back twenty-seven years later, I am struck by how rich God's promises have been to me and to my son. Apart from shuffling a deck of cards and excelling on the monkey bars in elementary school, David has been able to do everything God has given him to do. I can honestly say, "Knowing who you are in Christ with one hand is better than not knowing who you are in Christ with two hands."

In a scene in the movie *Shadowlands*, C. S. Lewis says concerning his wife's battle with cancer, "I pray because I can't help myself. I pray because I'm helpless."

Most people feel guilty because they don't pray enough. I gave up that attitude years ago. God can't be pleased when our conversation with him is out of obligation rather than out of our desire and an utter desperation for help and guidance.

Do we dare take to heart the challenge of these Scriptures on prayer and allow them to also flow out through our actions as we speak to God in reverence and worship, and also as we enjoy the deep intimacy of a relationship with a Friend we know loves us and we him?

In the Gospel accounts, we see Jesus take every key decision and event in his life to his Father. He came to accomplish the Father's purposes, so he received his direction and strength from those intimate times of communication. The same will be true of us. We must pray as Jesus prayed. Prayer is the practice creating the vital connection between God's heart and ours.

The writer of Hebrews points us to the joy of this practice of prayer: "Let us then approach God's throne of grace with confidence, so that we may receive mercy and find grace to help us in our time of need" (Hebrews 4:16).

Bible Study

For the word of God is alive and active. Sharper than any double-edged sword, it penetrates even to dividing soul and spirit, joints and marrow; it judges the thoughts and attitudes of the heart.

HEBREWS 4:12

The writer of the letter to the Hebrews teaches by analogy that Scripture is more powerful than any sword, yet it works in much the same way. For as you hold God's Word before you while moving through life, it can cut through any and every issue, dividing each into good and evil, righteous and wrong, showing us what we are to do and how to live. Like a sword, God's Word can be used as an offensive weapon in helping us to grow and mature, as well as a defensive device in helping to protect us against oncoming evil.

KEY QUESTION: How do I study God's Word?

We study God's Word with the intent of letting it guide our very lives, just as Jesus did, as recorded in Matthew 4:1 – 11:

> Then Jesus was led by the Spirit into the wilderness to be tempted by the devil. After fasting forty days and forty nights, he was hungry. The tempter came to him and said, "If you are the Son of God, tell these stones to become bread."
> Jesus answered, "It is written: 'Man shall not live on bread alone, but on every word that comes from the mouth of God.'"

> *Then the devil took him to the holy city and had him stand on the highest point of the temple. "If you are the Son of God," he said, "throw yourself down. For it is written:*
>
> *" 'He will command his angels concerning you,*
> *and they will lift you up in their hands,*
> *so that you will not strike your foot against a stone.' "*
>
> *Jesus answered him, "It is also written: 'Do not put the Lord your God to the test.' "*
>
> *Again, the devil took him to a very high mountain and showed him all the kingdoms of the world and their splendor. "All this I will give you," he said, "if you will bow down and worship me."*
>
> *Jesus said to him, "Away from me, Satan! For it is written: 'Worship the Lord your God, and serve him only.' "*
>
> *Then the devil left him, and angels came and attended him.*

Jesus responded to Satan's temptations with only words from the book of Deuteronomy.

Satan's temptation #1: Entice Jesus into performing a miracle to meet his own physical needs.

Jesus' response (Deuteronomy 8:3, italics added to show the words from Deuteronomy):

> He humbled you, causing you to hunger and then feeding you with manna, which neither you nor your ancestors had known, to *teach you that man does not live on bread alone but on every word that comes from the mouth of the* LORD.

Satan's temptation #2: Lure Jesus into asking God for proof of his love and care for him, out of a completely selfish act.

Jesus' response (Deuteronomy 6:16, italics added to show the words from Deuteronomy):

> *Do not put the* LORD *your God to the test as you did at Massah.*

Satan's temptation #3: Induce Jesus to serve him, as well as join him in authority over all Satan's access to the stuff of earth.

Jesus' response (Deuteronomy 6:13, italics added to show the words from Deuteronomy):

> Fear the LORD your God, serve him only *and take your oaths in his name.*

In temptation #2, Satan quoted Psalm 91:11 – 12 to Jesus, proving that he, too, knows and can use the Word. But he has shown he will only use it against God for his own selfish purposes.

Note also that the temptations grew in their scope as each one failed — from personal needs to protection to greed. Satan was, in effect, "zooming out" from inward appetite to outside influence. If Jesus battled his archenemy with only the Word of God, then as his children, we should also make this our only "sword" of defense to defeat him. But to *wield* his Word, we must *know* his Word, as Jesus so succinctly showed us how to do.

Jesus also frequently quoted from Old Testament passages in his teaching. In one of his postresurrection appearances to his disciples, he ties himself directly to Scripture and the revelation of its words:

> He said to them, "This is what I told you while I was still with you: Everything must be fulfilled that is written about me in the Law of Moses, the Prophets and the Psalms."
> Then he opened their minds so they could understand the Scriptures (Luke 24:44 – 45).

Jesus not only authored the Scriptures; he came to fulfill and live out every page. Seeing his constant intertwining of the Word into his ministry shows us the vital importance of knowing, understanding, memorizing, and applying the Bible.

KEY IDEA: I study the Bible to know God and his truth and to find direction for my daily life.

While your Bible may look like a book that contains paper and ink, Scripture tells us it is alive with God's own breath. His words are not dormant on a page, but active in the lives of those who will consume and apply them.

The believer who attempts to live the Christian life with their Bible gathering dust is like a construction worker trying to build a skyscraper without blueprints. What is the point without the plan?

God's Word cuts to the core, acting much like a surgeon's scalpel, exposing what is in our minds for him to do the work in us that only our Creator can do. It gets under our skin, below the surface, to expose our true motives and to reveal the truth to our spirit.

As sinners, we can deceive ourselves, as well as the people around us, with what is truly in our hearts, but the Bible shows us who we actually are, judging our true beliefs. As we read, soak in, and apply its truths, Scripture performs spiritual open-heart surgery. Like a personal counselor, God's Word can go straight to the source of our issues, connecting with and changing our actions, our thoughts, and even our very motives.

KEY APPLICATION: What difference does this make in the way I live?

- We regularly read and study God's Word.
- We come to see that studying God's Word in community with other believers is of great value.
- We align our lives to the Bible because we believe it is from God.

We must go to the Scriptures regularly, because God's Word has the right to invade and permeate our lives. When we consistently read its pages, we declare and prove we believe what is found there. Bible study will strongly reinforce every belief. In its pages, we find God; we learn how we are saved; we discover who we are in him; we are shown how to engage and govern his church; we gain insight into what it means to be a steward; we are taught what eternity will be like; we see how much God cares and loves his creation — and we receive thousands of precepts, promises, and principles.

Along with Old and New Testament writers, we acknowledge God's greatness and the power of his Word:

> "Who has gone up to heaven and come down?
>   Whose hands have gathered up the wind?
> Who has wrapped up the waters in a cloak?
>   Who has established all the ends of the earth?
> What is his name, and what is the name of his son?
>   Surely you know!
> Every word of God is flawless;
>   he is a shield to those who take refuge in him"
>   (Proverbs 30:4–5).

> And we also thank God continually because, when you received the word of God, which you heard from us, you accepted it not as a human word, but as it actually is, the word of God, which is indeed at work in you who believe (1 Thessalonians 2:13).

Consider this: What if for one week you exchanged your mobile phone for your Bible? Anywhere you normally take your phone, you take your Bible instead. Anytime you normally look at your phone, you look at God's Word instead. The time you spend calling, texting, and browsing online with your phone is traded for time reading Scripture. If you normally place your phone next to you at a business meeting or by your plate at dinnertime, you now put your Bible there. What difference would this exchange make in your life in just one week? Whose life would be impacted? This line of questions is not intended to trigger guilt, but rather to inspire us to increase our engagement with the one instrument that can truly change not only our lives but the lives of those around us.

As you practice the study of the Bible, God wants to work his Word in and through your life:

"If you work the words into your life, you are like a smart carpenter who dug deep and laid the foundation of his house on bedrock. When the river burst its banks and crashed against the house, nothing could shake it; it was built to last" (Luke 6:48 MSG).

Single-Mindedness

"But seek first his kingdom and his righteousness, and all these things will be given to you as well."

MATTHEW 6:33

Because of our sinful nature and self-centeredness, we often start an endeavor with the mind-set of what we want and then ask God to bless it — treating him like a sort of cosmic Santa Claus and expecting our wishes to be fulfilled. This makes life about us, not him — about our will, not his.

Matthew 6:33 inspires a fully submitted relationship in which God, his ways, and his plan are put first on a daily basis, trusting he will do the absolute best for us in any circumstance. While what he does is always right for us, we will certainly not always agree with how he allows life to play out. This is where faith makes all the difference. Keeping our focus on "his kingdom and his righteousness" is what we mean by being single-minded.

It is vital to understand what the phrase "these things" means in the second half of verse 33. We must look at verses 25 – 32 to gain context.

"I tell you, do not worry about your life, what you will eat or drink; or about your body, what you will wear. Is not life more than food, and the body more than clothes? Look at the birds of the air; they do not sow or reap or store away in barns, and yet your heavenly Father feeds them. Are you not much more valuable than they? Can any one of you by worrying add a single hour to your life?

"And why do you worry about clothes? See how the flowers of the field grow. They do not labor or spin. Yet I tell you that not even Solomon in all his splendor was dressed like one of these. If that is how God clothes the grass of the field, which is here today and tomorrow is thrown into the fire, will he not much more clothe you — you of little faith? So do not worry, saying, 'What shall we eat?' or 'What shall we drink?' or 'What shall we wear?' For the pagans run after all these things, and your heavenly Father knows that you need them."

Jesus is letting us know he is well aware of what we need, if we will simply depend on him to provide. Dependence on him is a precursor to single-mindedness — which leads us to verse 34: "Therefore do not worry about tomorrow, for tomorrow will worry about itself. Each day has enough trouble of its own."

Jesus knows that a single-minded person will live each day yielded to God's will and direction, just as he modeled for us in his three years of ministry. Jesus placed God's will first, and he was provided for; so we can also trust he will do the same for us, his children.

Ever heard the old saying, "You can't have your cake and eat it too"? Well, this may well be one of the only situations in life where this statement is *in*correct, because once we surrender to God, we receive an abundant life here *and* the gift of eternal life in heaven.

KEY QUESTION: How do I keep my focus on Jesus amid distractions?

Single-mindedness points to and permeates all the key beliefs to think like Jesus. Let me cite just a few examples:

1. He is God, and I am not. The focus of my life is on him.
   (BELIEF: God)

2. The authority of the Bible has my attention and outlines my priorities. (BELIEF: Bible)

3. My priorities come from the Owner of life.
   (BELIEF: Stewardship)

Jesus is the ultimate model of what single-mindedness looks like. John records this statement of Jesus: "'My food,' said Jesus, 'is to do the will of him who sent me and to finish his work'" (John 4:34). If we are to act like him, we must increasingly surrender our minds and hearts to his will.

KEY IDEA: I focus on God and his priorities for my life.

A good place to start in putting God first is to evaluate and target areas where we may not be seeking him. Here's an exercise to help you do this. At the end of a day, take a few minutes to think back through your activities. Try to recall your thought processes as well. If someone had shadowed you all day, what might they say you were seeking? What would a stranger see you place first in your life? What were you focused on? Exactly what were your priorities?

Here is the startling great news about a relationship with God: He will never say to any of us, "Well, I met someone else ..." or "I just don't think this is working out." He is all-in, 24/7/365, and is constantly pursuing us. He seeks us all the time — forever.

The great challenge for us is to remain faithful to him. Yet when we fail, and we will, we can seek forgiveness and move right back into relationship with him.

As we mature in our belief, an ever-growing desire should be to simply love and seek the One who promises to never leave or forsake us — not because we want more blessings or favor, but solely because he is worthy of our full focus and attention. This is another strong indicator of single-mindedness.

Pursuing God as the very first thing — before anything else — is a clear mission statement. When we get to that frequent questioning point of "What is God's will for my life?" Matthew 6:33

provides a steady answer to this question. Single-mindedness is the answer in our search.

Unlike an earthly king's physical realm, God's kingdom is only visible in the lives of his followers who are doing the very thing we are talking about — seeking him first. Earthly kings have borders and boundaries; God does not. His kingdom is found in his people and his activity. As his temples, wherever we move, his kingdom is represented.

KEY APPLICATION: What difference does this make in the way I live?

- We set goals informed by God's agenda and will.
- We don't ask God to bless our plan but to bless our alignment to *his* plan.
- We trust God to meet our needs and desires.

God makes a profound promise to us in Matthew 6:33 and offers a great blessing for being single-minded. He promises that if we will take care of his business here on earth, he will take care of us both here and in eternity. In short — we take care of his kingdom, and he'll take care of ours.

Who else could offer you such an amazing deal?

In December 2006, eighteen-year-old Katie Davis of Brentwood, Tennessee, traveled to Uganda for the first time. She had no idea that the very course of her life would be changed on the trip and that her life would take on a razor-sharp focus in one small corner of the world. In 2007, Katie returned to Uganda to teach kindergarten at an orphanage. She was surprised by the number of children sitting on the side of the road or working in the fields. There were no government-run public schools in the area of Uganda where she was living. Most schools are privately operated and require fees for attendance, making it unaffordable for children to get an education.

Katie began a child sponsorship program that matched orphaned children with sponsors to provide education funding, school supplies, daily hot meals, spiritual discipleship, and medical care. By January 2008, Katie had brought 150 kids into the program. To date, over 600 children are now in her care. She also started a program in the Karimojong community that feeds more than 1,200 children. They also receive schooling, medical care, Bible study, and health training.

Katie established a nonprofit organization called Amazima Ministries International to meet the physical, emotional, and spiritual needs of orphaned children in Uganda. In the Lugandan language, *amazima* means "truth."

In January 2008, Katie became the mother of three orphaned girls. Today, the mother of thirteen adopted daughters, she says, "People tell me I am brave. People tell me I am strong. People tell me 'good job.' Well, here is the truth of it. I am really not that brave, I am not really that strong, and I am not doing anything spectacular. I am just doing what God called me to do as a follower of him. Feed his sheep, do unto the least of his people."[22]

Young Katie Davis's life is a bright example of single-mindedness and the amazing blessing God can bring through its practice. She has no doubt when her feet hit the floor every morning that her life has divine purpose and meaning. She knows the truth of Jesus' teaching: "If you cling to your life, you will lose it, and if you let your life go, you will save it" (Luke 17:33 NLT).

As you practice single-mindedness, something begins to change within you. The words of the psalmist in Psalm 37:4 become true in your life:

> Take delight in the LORD,
>   and he will give you the desires of your heart.

The decision to follow God is difficult at first because his plan often conflicts with your plan. But when you first focus on God, he promises to give you the desires of your heart. Here's how it works.

As you go through the process of focusing on God, he changes the desires of your heart so that, over time, what you want for yourself mirrors what he wants for you.

No one can deny that our lifestyles today are chaotic and complex. Single-mindedness actually offers simplicity. Our lives can be uncluttered by the Creator and set on a path toward purpose and peace by his grace and mercy.

Total Surrender

I urge you, brothers and sisters, in view of God's mercy, to offer your bodies as a living sacrifice, holy and pleasing to God—this is your true and proper worship.

ROMANS 12:1

We are only able to strive for total surrender in our lives through God's wonderful gift of grace. This does not mean we give up our lives to him out of some obligation or debt in trade for redemption; nor does it mean giving up control because he has overpowered us. Rather we fully surrender to him out of total desperation and realization for the need of a Savior.

The first eleven chapters of the apostle Paul's letter to the Romans detail our need for mercy and God's gracious provision of mercy through Jesus. Now, as chapter 12 begins, he writes, "In view of God's mercy ..." As we consider this concept, we are left with an obvious response of total surrender to God's will. He should so capture our hearts for today and forever that we are compelled to give up our lives to him — from love, not duty; for worship, not works.

KEY QUESTION: How do I cultivate a life of sacrificial service?

Jesus practiced total surrender daily. He invites us to adopt this same lifestyle with his use of "all-in" language in the Gospels. For example, Jesus calls those who want to follow him to "lose their life" for him: "Then Jesus said to his disciples, 'Whoever wants to be my disciple must deny themselves and take up their cross and follow me. For whoever wants to save their life will lose it, but whoever loses their life for me will find it'" (Matthew 16:24–25).

In Luke's gospel, we are given examples of what total surrender does *not* look like: "As they [the disciples and Jesus] were walking along the road, a man said to him, "I will follow you wherever you go"' (Luke 9:57). Now, this man's declaration sounds like an impressive admission of total surrender, does it not? Shouldn't this bold statement excite Jesus and shouldn't this person be exactly the kind of follower he was looking for?

This was Jesus' response: "Foxes have dens and birds have nests, but the Son of Man has no place to lay his head" (Luke 9:58). And then in the next verse we see Jesus moving his attention to another man. What happened? We are left to assume this man was exercising lip service, not exhibiting submission to the Lord. As we reflect on this encounter, we ponder the truth that there is a high cost to living a life of total surrender (Luke 14:26–33).

Now, moving on to the second potential follower:

> He [Jesus] said to another man, "Follow me."
> But he replied, "Lord, first let me go and bury my father."
> Jesus said to him, "Let the dead bury their own dead, but you go and proclaim the kingdom of God" (Luke 9:59–60).

While at first blush Jesus' response sounds harsh, we must remember he was walking with men who had already left behind everything to follow him. His invitation was urgent and current, not a simple RSVP. Jesus' call was to spread the message of life, not to carry out the rites of death. His disciples were moving forward with the kingdom and the business of life.

There is a third and final man in this scene:

> Still another said, "I will follow you, Lord; but first let me go back and say goodbye to my family."

Jesus replied, "No one who puts a hand to the plow and looks back is fit for service in the kingdom of God" (Luke 9:61–62).

Once again, this may be a well-intentioned response from a potential disciple, if we give him the benefit of the doubt, but our takeaway from Jesus' response to both of these men is to realize that delayed obedience to God is really equivalent to disobedience. When he invites us into his work, the time is now, not later. The day of salvation is always today.

When Jesus was healing, performing miracles, and meeting needs, crowds of people appeared to be all-in. Yet when he made strong statements, such as in the verses above, about the reality of following him, many decided total surrender simply cost too much. By the time Jesus hung on the cross, even his closest friends had abandoned him. His final act of total surrender to the Father was completed alone. The road walked with Jesus is truly the narrow one he describes in Matthew 7:13 – 14.

KEY IDEA: I dedicate my life to God's purposes.

Agnes Gonxha Bojaxhiu's father died when she was only nine. As early as the age of twelve, Agnes felt called to a religious life. Although her mother was initially against the idea of her beloved daughter leaving her home in Macedonia to serve in India, she eventually understood the call of God and gave Agnes this piece of prophetic advice: "Put your hand in his hand and walk all alone with him."[23] This charge would mark her life for the rest of her days. Agnes, better known as Mother Teresa, died at the age of eighty-seven. Her efforts had produced fruit in over 130 countries, including a network of 600 homeless shelters, orphanages, AIDS hospices, leprosy clinics, and homes for single mothers. A Gallup Poll survey in 1999 named her No. 1 on the list of the most widely admired people of the twentieth century.[24]

The cultural norm will always be to fulfill our own desires as much as possible — which is the opposite of our key idea. Committing to hand over life to an unseen God not only will be unpopular; it will also make for some difficult days. Why? Because we are choosing to go against the grain of the self-centered human nature. But note our key idea has a goal and purpose — to dedicate our lives to God's purposes.

In Matthew 25, Jesus uses a metaphor about separating sheep from goats. In Scripture, believers are often compared to sheep. Here, Jesus uses this imagery while comparing unbelievers to goats. It is ironic to see the righteous group's response to his invitation of eternal inheritance.

> *"Then the righteous will answer him, 'Lord, when did we see you hungry and feed you, or thirsty and give you something to drink? When did we see you a stranger and invite you in, or needing clothes and clothe you? When did we see you sick or in prison and go to visit you?'"* (Matthew 25:37–39).

The righteous people are a bit confused, which leads them to pose some questions. They had no idea that when they were serving people, they were also serving Jesus — feeding, clothing, and caring for him — every time. Total surrender to Christ will result in these regular acts of love, not in isolated and rare incidents of self-directed humanitarian effort. And total surrender will elicit this response from the King: "Truly I tell you, whatever you did for one of the least of these brothers and sisters of mine, you did for me" (Matthew 25:40).

We must again repeat the greatest commandment, for its truth lies at the very heart of all the beliefs and practices of Jesus, but most especially the expression of this practice: "'Love the Lord your God with all your heart and with all your soul and with all your mind.' This is the first and greatest commandment. And the second is like it: 'Love your neighbor as yourself'" (Matthew 22:37–39).

The only way to live out Jesus' calling on our lives is through total surrender. As Mother Teresa's mother encouraged her, our Lord urges us to simply put our hand in his hand and walk all alone with him.

KEY APPLICATION: What difference does this make in the way I live?

We daily open our hands and surrender all we have to God.

The word *surrender* has been the subject of many classic hymns and continues to be a popular theme in modern worship songs. At the very mention of the word, you likely can break out into singing with a melody you know by heart. While the concept of surrender is quite familiar in most churches, the biblical connotation must be continually driven home to both remind and prompt us to daily "lay down" our blatant rebellion and self-centered agendas, while we "lift our hands" to abdicate control and give all authority to God.

To surrender means to give up the battle of the flesh, to give over control of your life, and to abandon your rights. The battle, control, and rights all come from the same place — the sinful nature. Declaring surrender is handing over your heart and life fully to Jesus, as you pray, *Lord, this is no longer my life, but yours; no longer my will, but yours; no longer my plan, but yours. I give my life to you, my life for you.*

We offer every moment, thought, and activity of our lives as a sacrifice to God.

I never tire of hearing the story of the chicken that shared with a pig his desire to prepare a special breakfast for their farmer. The chicken said to the pig, "I will provide the eggs, and you provide the bacon." The pig thought about it for a moment and then responded, "You are only making a contribution; I am making a total sacrifice!"

We should be willing to die for God, but he's not asking us to be a "dead sacrifice"; he wants us to be a "living sacrifice." Frankly, offering our lives as a dead sacrifice might be a bit easier. Someone once wisely said, "The problem with living sacrifices is they keep crawling off the altar."

In light of what God has done to give us life, we should offer ourselves as living sacrifices back to him.

We will serve God in any way he desires.

The first two application points have to do with the mind and heart uniting around a new life and identity. Service is the outward display of the new lifestyle. Yet, God is no drill sergeant, angrily barking out orders, or some cosmic slave master needing dirty work done. He walks with you as a friend and invites you to work with him as a team.

The Christian whose life is continually yielded to God in surrender, sacrifice, and service will be not only a living witness but also a world changer.

To totally surrender, submitting to Christ's authority and dedicating our lives to his service, will bring us into the company of some of the greatest humans to ever walk the planet — the heroes of our faith (see Hebrews 11:1 – 12:3). Let us echo the words of one of those — the apostle Paul — as we close:

> I consider my life worth nothing to me; my only aim is to finish the race and complete the task the Lord Jesus has given me—the task of testifying to the good news of God's grace (Acts 20:24).

Biblical Community

All the believers were together and had everything in common. They sold property and possessions to give to anyone who had need. Every day they continued to meet together in the temple courts. They broke bread in their homes and ate together with glad and sincere hearts, praising God and enjoying the favor of all the people. And the Lord added to their number daily those who were being saved.

ACTS 2:44 – 47

Scripture makes it clear through commands, promises, and examples that the Christian life was never intended to be lived alone. Those who have received Christ are now wired through their new spiritual DNA to live in community. We must have a band of believers to walk alongside us, all pointed in the same direction — toward the Father. Only collectively are we the body of Christ. We need each other to help us become like Jesus and consistently model his life.

KEY QUESTION: How do I develop healthy relationships with others?

In Genesis 1 and other Scripture passages, we see the Trinity is, in itself, a community. Three persons — Father, Son, and Holy Spirit — who are so intense and complete in their unity that they make up one essence. We are made in his image to experience this same community. Separate in entity, one in unity. The apostle Paul reminds us of our common bond:

> *There is one body and one Spirit, just as you were called to one hope when you were called; one Lord, one faith, one baptism; one God and Father of all, who is over all and through all and in all (Ephesians 4:4–6).*

> *If you have any encouragement from being united with Christ, if any comfort from his love, if any common sharing in the Spirit, if any tenderness and compassion, then make my joy complete by being like-minded, having the same love, being one in spirit and of one mind (Philippians 2:1–2).*

As you have read the accounts of Jesus' calling his disciples at the beginning of his ministry, have you ever thought about his recruitment style? What was his end goal? Since he is God, he could easily have walked down the beach and assembled an army of 12,000 men to overthrow the government. He could have called together 1,200 and given them amazing powers. But he did nothing of the sort. In fact, he didn't even call 120. Essentially, Jesus formed the very first "small group," as they're called in the church today. He launched his ministry with 12 men. He put together a tiny community of very diverse and, frankly, mostly unimpressive followers. Why? Because Jesus wasn't planning a coup or forming a cult; rather, he was building a community.

He didn't call those he chose based on résumé, IQ, or brawn. The fact that his original small group formed the church that still lives today shows he chose wisely as he prepared a body of believers to carry out his work — which swept through the known world after his ascension into heaven.

KEY IDEA: I fellowship with Christians to accomplish God's purposes in my life, in the life of others, and in the world.

The book of Acts contains a passage that beautifully displays the simple power of community to which we are called, while also highlighting the critical commitment we must make as individuals:

In Joppa there was a disciple named Tabitha (in Greek her name is Dorcas); she was always doing good and helping the poor. About that time she became sick and died, and her body was washed and placed in an upstairs room. Lydda was near Joppa; so when the disciples heard that Peter was in Lydda, they sent two men to him and urged him, "Please come at once!"

Peter went with them, and when he arrived he was taken upstairs to the room. All the widows stood around him, crying and showing him the robes and other clothing that Dorcas had made while she was still with them.

Peter sent them all out of the room; then he got down on his knees and prayed. Turning toward the dead woman, he said, "Tabitha, get up." She opened her eyes, and seeing Peter she sat up. He took her by the hand and helped her to her feet. Then he called for the believers, especially the widows, and presented her to them alive. This became known all over Joppa, and many people believed in the Lord (Acts 9:36–42).

Tabitha was a widow who had become a vital part of the body of believers, as she was "always doing good and helping the poor" — so much so that the people missed her deeply and sent messengers to summon Peter, hoping he could do something. Miraculously, through the power of God, Peter knelt and prayed, and Tabitha came back to life!

It is important to see that the degree to which Tabitha had *given* her life to biblical community was, in the end, the very motivation of Peter to *extend* her life. She had made herself so integral to these fellow believers that they wouldn't take death as the final answer. This account of a widow who lived sacrificially provides inspiration for us to graft ourselves deeply into a body of believers to make this kind of difference.

To properly define biblical community, look no further than the last few syllables in the phrase — "unity." This is both the point and practice of the concept.

Christ's vision is that you will become an integral part of his grand body of believers, ushering in his kingdom around the globe by being grafted into the lives of a local body, making a difference right where you are. The ministry you do for a neighbor truly does impact the world as all believers join in obeying Christ. This is a sort of "one for all, and all for one" battle cry.

The practice of biblical community reinforces both our belief in our identity in Christ individually and our belief in the church to, together, be his hands and feet to the world.

KEY APPLICATION: What difference does this make in the way I live?

"You become who you hang out with."

"Show me your friends, and I'll show you your future."

These are just two of a number of catchphrases that describe the impact of those with whom we spend the most time. The book of Proverbs contains many verses that attach the impact of our relationships to the development of our identity.

We fellowship with other believers to keep our relationship with God strong.

Biblical community will, first, keep our vertical connection — our relationship with God — strong. Nothing will hold us accountable and encourage us to follow Jesus quite like other Christ followers. The effect of us joining in the mission to "spur one another on toward love and good deeds" is powerful (Hebrews 10:24).

We fellowship with other believers to keep our relationships with others strong.

Biblical community is the optimum way to keep our horizontal relationships on the right and righteous path. Fellow Christians can help us strengthen our ties to those in the church and outside the church. We can together encourage and build each other up inside the body, while praying for and challenging each other to reach out to those who don't know Christ.

We fellowship with other believers to accomplish God's will on earth.

If you were going to rescue a person who had fallen off a steep cliff, you would want to be tied to as many people up on the mountain as possible, supporting you and holding you as you attempt rescue. As we minister and reach out to those outside the community of faith, it is necessary to stay tethered together for optimum success, lest we also fall.

There are days we desperately need a good hug to keep going, and other days we need a swift kick in the pants to get back to where we should be. Friends who love God, and love us for who we are, know exactly when and how to do the right thing for us. In the book of Proverbs, Solomon writes, "Faithful are the wounds of a friend" (Proverbs 27:6 NKJV).

Biblical community is the glue holding us together, through which we have opportunity to grow in favor with God and to keep our relationships right with others. Are you struggling in your relationship with God? Do you find yourself simply wanting to love him more than you do? Are you finding yourself in continual dysfunction with those around you? Or do you desire to strengthen your relationships to a greater degree? Connecting to, submitting with, and walking alongside brothers and sisters in Christ can get you on the right track, while also keeping you on the path to God's truth and his will.

Spiritual Gifts

> For just as each of us has one body with many members,
> and these members do not all have the same function,
> so in Christ we, though many, form one body, and each
> member belongs to all the others. We have different gifts,
> according to the grace given to each of us.
>
> ROMANS 12:4–6

When we made a courageous decision to step across the line of faith and embrace God's offer of salvation through the grace and mercy of Christ, the Holy Spirit deposited a spiritual gift or gifts. These are offered out of God's treasury of righteous qualities. We do not have to ask him; he gives them freely from his Father heart.

When the Creator forms us in the womb, he molds and shapes our personality and abilities, and he also gives us talents to use for our personal satisfaction and the benefit of the world. If someone can mesmerize audiences with his or her singing voice, amaze with intellectual inventions of architecture or fashion, or excite with an athletic ability, these have been placed in the body and soul from conception. These talents and skills can certainly be used for God's glory, but millions of people use them only for personal glory. When someone becomes a Christian, God repurposes the innate talents he created in that person at birth to be used to accomplish his purposes through his church. But it is also true that God deposits a spiritual gift (or gifts) in a person when the Holy Spirit takes up residence in him or her. This gift, along with the uniqueness of their personality and the talents given at their birth, are used for a high and eternal purpose.

KEY QUESTION: What gifts and abilities has God given me to serve others?

How can we then know our gifts? Let me give you a scenario to consider.

Imagine driving down the freeway. In front of your vehicle is a pickup truck with a family of five inside. In the back of the truck are a number of cages filled with chickens. The truck suddenly begins to swerve, out of control, runs off the road into the ditch, and flips over. The cages fly out the back and break open, and all the chickens are released. You, along with a number of others, immediately pull off on the shoulder to help.

Now, I want you to think about your first response and the activity you would most likely engage in as you stop to assist at this scene.

Are you the person who would immediately take charge? You would announce to everyone, "I've got this figured out, people. Just leave it to me, and listen up." You begin delegating responsibilities and giving orders as bystanders spring into action.

Are you the person who would begin to organize and oversee the details? After hearing the orders from the leader, you start to implement the plan. You divide people into groups and distribute equipment — someone to direct traffic, those who would assist the victims, and those who would be the chicken wranglers. You then make sure those groups have the necessary tools to get the job done.

Are you the person who would focus completely on the needs of the people? Forget the truck. The chickens can wait. You go straight to the five people in the vehicle to offer them assistance, put them at ease, and care for them until the paramedics arrive. A sense of mercy for the victims is your primary focus.

Are you the person who quickly realizes this effort is going to take a while? The rescue team is going to need food and water, so you take off to grab some supplies. Your need to be hospitable to those who are sacrificing time and energy calls you to service.

Are you the person who would begin to ask the people around the accident what everyone might learn from this unfortunate situation? What could have been done to avoid the loss of control? How can this be prevented in the future? What steps should the highway department take to avoid another accident at this location? You desire to gather the intel to teach others to avoid such an accident in the future.

Are you the person who simply walks up and asks, "Hey, how can I help? Put me to work. Whatever you need me to do, I'll do." Then you stay and do the dirty work until the victims have been taken to the hospital and every chicken has been re-caged. Before you leave, you even pick up the debris from the accident after the tow truck driver hauls the vehicle away.

Do you see the different gifts engaged and actions taken by people who all encounter the same problem? The role you see yourself as taking on in this setting can indicate a great deal about the spiritual gift God has given you.

As in the case of those on the scene of the hypothetical accident, your gift has not been given for your own personal benefit, but rather is to be used to serve in concert with other members of the body of Christ.

KEY IDEA: I know my spiritual gifts and use them to fulfill God's purposes.

Consider this accident scenario again. I listed six gifting possibilities. What if a person to match each gift had stopped to help? What if six people had shown up, each representing one of these gifts? Everything involved in this accident — the victims, the chickens, the truck, and the traffic — would be well covered, wouldn't it? Therein lies God's intention for us to meet needs on the earth. We work together for his glory.

When you became a member of the body of Christ, you joined a community of people who are under the authority and guidance of God himself. The contribution of your gift will accomplish his purposes for the advancement of the kingdom. In Romans 12:3 – 8, the apostle Paul writes:

> By the grace given me I say to every one of you: Do not think of yourself more highly than you ought, but rather think of yourself with sober judgment, in accordance with the faith God has distributed to each of you. For just as each of us has one body with many members, and these members do not all have the same function, so in Christ we, though many, form one body, and each member belongs to all the others. We have different gifts, according to the grace given to each of us. If your gift is prophesying, then prophesy in accordance with your faith; if it is serving, then serve; if it is teaching, then teach; if it is to encourage, then give encouragement; if it is giving, then give generously; if it is to lead, do it diligently; if it is to show mercy, do it cheerfully.

Our spiritual gifts are to be practiced out of a heart of grace, humility, and faith. We are commissioned to discover what God has gifted us with and to use it for his glory and the benefit of the world. Essentially, Paul tells us in straightforward language to find our gift and then give it away!

KEY APPLICATION: What difference does this make in the way I live?

- We seek to serve, using our gifts to glorify God and help others.
- We value and respect the gifts of others as together we serve God's purposes.
- We come to see that using our gifts for God gives us a purpose bigger than ourselves.

As with biblical community, spiritual gifts strongly affect your relationship with God and with others.

Let's address our gifts' impact on others. But first a question: Why would God only give us one or two of these gifts rather than give every gift to us all? He certainly could do such a thing. The answer connects us back to biblical community. He wants us to rely on each other and cooperate with each other. Our limitations in the gifts create a need for interdependence, for our brothers and sisters to share with the community their gifts, as well as to keep us humble, because we cannot reach the world alone.

As a seeking, hurting world watches us cooperate and move in unison to meet needs, they will be drawn to want to experience the life-changing power of shunning the "every man for himself" attitude and embracing the "every soul matters" mission of Jesus.

Since the Holy Spirit has given these gifts, he will guide as to their use. He knows exactly what is needed, when it is needed, and where it is needed. Therefore, listening to and obeying the Lord become vital responses for using spiritual gifts. This ongoing process continually strengthens and hones our connection to the Father.

We clearly see this interaction at work in Paul's words to the Corinthian church: "What, after all, is Apollos? And what is Paul? Only servants, through whom you came to believe — as the Lord has assigned to each his task. I planted the seed, Apollos watered it, but God has been making it grow" (1 Corinthians 3:5 – 6).

If you want to gain a better understanding of your own spiritual gifts, look for a number of excellent resources and tools online or in Christian bookstores. You can also simply ask people to help you discover your gifts. Use the story in this chapter and ask three folks to circle the role they see you playing. Your responsibility is to discover and develop God's gifts, and then to find how each one fits into the world he wants to reach. You have been given a gift, and God plans to use your gift to change the world.

When we are children, most of us pretend to have, or dream about having, some sort of superpower. The Creator has given you a divine gift. When it is used in and through your unique personality, abilities, and intellect, energized by his Holy Spirit, God will certainly produce supernatural results far above what you could ask for or imagine him to ever do.

Offering My Time

Whatever you do, whether in word or deed, do it all in the name of the Lord Jesus, giving thanks to God the Father through him.

COLOSSIANS 3:17

Most of us consider Monday morning to be the start of our week, and Sunday night the end. And then we start another week all over again. The rotation of the clock continues for us all. Here is a quite interesting fact about our time, which is different from so many other resources in our lives: We all are given exactly the same amount of this gift! There are seven days in a week and there are 24 hours in each day — 7 x 24 = 168. We all get 168 hours every single week. We have no choice. We can't buy or barter for more time, and we can't decide to take less. We do, however, have the choice as to how we use each hour. For this reason, time is, indeed, a precious commodity, as well as an equalizing factor, for all mankind. None of us can offer any excuse for productivity or any priority for having less or more. The real question then becomes this: How do we use this finite resource called time?

KEY QUESTION: How do I best use my time to serve God and others?

The Bible teaches in many passages about our use of time. Colossians 3:17 is particularly helpful for reminding us that our daily schedules should look much different now than they did before our salvation: "Whatever you do, whether in word or deed, do it all in the name of the Lord Jesus, giving thanks to God the Father through him."

Jesus' new life in us should change our priorities and how we view the gift of time. Simply put, our calendars must be redeemed not long after our souls are redeemed.

Why else would anyone want to spend their day off helping a widow down the street with repairs on her house?

Why else would anyone assist a single mom by watching her kids while she goes to buy groceries?

Why else would anyone want to mentor an at-risk student once a week?

Why else would anyone want to volunteer in the church nursery?

These are but a few examples of what giving time back to Christ looks like.

KEY IDEA: I offer my time to fulfill God's purposes.

When Jesus hung on the cross, he made his sacrifice all about us. But we are now set free from living self-focused lives, so we can be engaged in the lives of others he deeply loves. Our time is no longer all about us, but is about Christ. It is not our time, but God's. His great love now motivates us to devote our schedule to serving his priorities.

We must be just as certain we are committed to the second half of this key idea as we are to the first. We must not only give away time but also use those hours to fulfill God's purposes, not our own or someone else's. This is the concept stated in Colossians 3:17. The person sentenced by a judge to community service as punishment for a crime is, in essence, "giving away his or her time"; the end goal, however, is not for the glory of God. As Christians, fulfilling God's plan and purpose with our time is just as crucial as giving the hours away.

Because of our response to God's great love and grace, we shouldn't need a law to tell us to give of our time to serve him. The proper response is being so overwhelmed by his sacrifice that we give of this precious resource to reach out in his name. It is one thing to have a spiritual gift, but it is quite another to allocate the hours to use a gift regularly for others and for the glory of God. With Paul, we rejoice in making this our testimony:

I have been crucified with Christ and I no longer live, but Christ lives in me. The life I now live in the body, I live by faith in the Son of God, who loved me and gave himself for me (Galatians 2:20).

KEY APPLICATION: What difference does this make in the way I live?

While offering your time to fulfill God's purposes is a straightforward concept, here are some suggestions to help you plan and prioritize.

1. Keep a log of your schedule for a week. The Notes app on your smartphone is a great place to do this. Be careful to avoid being too generic. Don't just write down "8 hours at work." This exercise intends for you to be specific by identifying where and how hours are used. At the end of the week, honestly answer these questions:

1. Does my schedule reflect how God wants me to use my time?
2. What adjustments should I make?
3. Where am I allowing room for temptation or sin?
4. Is there an activity I believe God is calling me to stop or delay?
5. Is there an activity I believe God is calling me to add to my schedule?
6. Where can I make more room for the use of my spiritual gift?

2. Use your daily drive time to call friends and check on them. This is especially useful for connecting with family and friends who live out of town — folks you don't get a chance to see regularly.

3. Seek out a ministry opportunity during your lunch hour or some other block of time that you could consistently make available for serving others. Look for small blocks of time you might not even realize you are wasting, which could easily be used for kingdom purposes. As you do so, you will be echoing the prayer of the psalmist:

> Teach us to number our days,
> that we may gain a heart of wisdom (Psalm 90:12).

4. Unite the practice of prayer with the practice of offering your time. Ask God to show you how to use your time wisely and in such a way that it brings glory to him.

- As you pray for God's guidance, he will help you *manage* time. The author of Ecclesiastes writes, "There is a time for everything, and a season for every activity under the heavens" (Ecclesiastes 3:1). As a steward of your life and manager of all God has given you, placing your calendar on the altar and offering it to the Lord is a great step of obedience to true lordship. His omniscience allows him to know exactly where you are and where you should be, what you are doing and what you should be doing, the people you are with and the people you should be with. All this he can tell you at any moment of the day. Giving him full access to speak to you at any time regarding your calendar will make all the difference as you serve in his name in your little corner of the world.

- As you pray for God's guidance, he will help you *multiply* time. In the book of Proverbs, we read, "Wisdom will multiply your days and add years to your life" (Proverbs 9:11 NLT). God has an amazing way of multiplying any resource given to him (remember the feeding of the five thousand!). In a way similar to what happened when the boy offered the loaves and fish, the more you commit your hours to him, the more your life will count and have an impact on people (see John 6:5 – 13). Just as time spent with no regard to God is quickly and easily wasted, time surrendered to him is made to count for all eternity.

- As you pray for God's guidance, he will help you *maximize* time. The author of Job tells us, "A person's days are determined; you have decreed the number of his months and have set limits he cannot exceed" (Job 14:5). While multiplying and maximizing may seem similar, multiplying is completely up to God. You give; he multiplies. Maximizing your time is a joint and synergetic effort between your focused obedience and his favored omniscience. What if every morning or each night you prayed, *Father, my time is yours. Show me, lead me, speak to me about what you want me to do, about how to use this precious gift wisely*, and then you listened, trusted, and obeyed?

Our work often causes us to focus on monetizing our time. The following story helps us understand the crucial need to both maximize and multiply our precious hours.

A man had been working very long hours for quite some time. One evening, he came home late again, exhausted, to find his five-year-old son waiting up for him. "Daddy, can I ask you a question?"

"Sure, I guess. What is it?" replied the dad.

"How much money do you make in an hour?"

Tired and irritated, he snapped, "What makes you ask such a thing?"

The son answered, "I just need to know. Please tell me, how much do you make in an hour?"

"Well, I make twenty dollars an hour."

Looking up toward his father, the boy asked, "Daddy, may I borrow ten dollars, please?"

The father was now furious. "If the only reason you wanted to know how much money I make is just so you can buy a toy or some other nonsense, then you march yourself straight to your room and go to bed. I work long, hard hours every day, and I don't have time for this right now." The little boy quietly went to his room and shut the door.

After a bit, the dad calmed down and began to think he may have been too hard on his son. Maybe he really did need the ten dollars for some good reason. He went to the door of his little boy's room. The dad asked, "Are you asleep, son?"

"No, Daddy, I'm awake," replied the boy.

"I've been thinking maybe I was too hard on you earlier," said the man. "It's been a long day, and I took out my frustrations on you. Here's ten dollars. What do you need it for?"

The little boy sat straight up. "Oh, thank you, Daddy!" Reaching under his pillow, he pulled out some crumpled bills he had saved from his allowance.

"Why did you want more money if you already had some?" the father asked, about to get irritated again.

The son slowly counted out his money and then, looking up at his dad, said, "Because I didn't have enough, but now I do. Daddy, I have twenty dollars now. Can I buy an hour of your time? I miss you."

While this story certainly tugs at our heartstrings and causes us to evaluate our own priorities of time, we cannot help but think of and be grateful for our heavenly Father, who gives us his constant, undivided, and unending attention to the details of our lives.

The psalmist David reminds us of the fragility of life and the importance of using our time wisely:

> Show me, LORD, my life's end
>   and the number of my days;
>   let me know how fleeting my life is.
> You have made my days a mere handbreadth;
>   the span of my years is as nothing before you.

Everyone is but a breath,
   even those who seem secure.
Surely everyone goes around like a mere phantom;
   in vain they rush about, heaping up wealth
   without knowing whose it will finally be.
But now, LORD, what do I look for?
   My hope is in you (Psalm 39:4–7).

Have you ever responded to someone who asked for a minute of your time by saying, "Sure, my time is your time"? Let this be our response to Jesus every day.

Giving My Resources

Since you excel in everything—in faith, in speech, in knowledge, in complete earnestness and in the love we have kindled in you—see that you also excel in this grace of giving.

2 CORINTHIANS 8:7

For children, there is a big difference between "have to" and "get to." "You have to go to the doctor for a shot." "You have to wait here and be quiet until I'm done." "You get to go out for ice cream." "You get to pick out a toy at the store because you were so patient." Early on, we learn to draw a line to divide activities we perceive to be fun or boring, good or bad, positive or negative.

As adults, we still experience plenty of "have to's" and "get to's" in life. But some of these areas can move from one extreme to the other, depending on the person and their circumstances. Giving certainly fits such a description—particularly giving to the church. One person finds great joy in giving regularly to support the gospel ministry, while another views it as a heavy burden. But what marks the difference in the two perspectives? What draws the line between joy and drudgery or delineates the boundary between generosity and greed?

KEY QUESTION: How do I best use my resources to serve God and others?

Historians tell us when soldiers in the Middle Ages came to faith in Christ and were baptized, the event often came with a unique twist. The warrior would keep his right arm up out of the water. The symbolic point intended was that the arm used for wielding his sword and killing would not be committed and surrendered to the Lord, as was the rest of his body. This decision was certainly an odd attempt to show that the left hand didn't know what the right hand was doing.

Today it seems many Christians hold their right arms out of the water as well — but with their wallet or purse in hand, as if to say, "Lord, you can have everything … except my money!" In his first letter to Timothy, Paul warns:

> Those who want to get rich fall into temptation and a trap and into many foolish and harmful desires that plunge people into ruin and destruction. For the love of money is a root of all kinds of evil. Some people, eager for money, have wandered from the faith and pierced themselves with many griefs (1 Timothy 6:9–10).

Of the thirty-eight parables of Jesus in the Bible, sixteen of them deal with how to handle possessions; all told, 288 verses in the Gospels — one out of every ten — refer to money. Over two thousand Bible verses talk about our personal resources, compared with approximately five hundred on prayer and fewer than five hundred on faith.[25] We can't conclude from these statistics that Jesus' heart was focused on money, but rather that he knew ours would be. His teaching continually directs us toward using all we have — including our money and our possessions — to love him and love others.

KEY IDEA: I give my resources to fulfill God's purposes.

God's great grace should move us to feel, not as though we are required to give, but as though we are privileged to give. The apostle Paul writes, "Each of you should give what you have decided in your heart to give, not reluctantly or under compulsion, for God loves a cheerful giver" (2 Corinthians 9:7).

As devoted followers of Christ, our daily prayer becomes, *Lord, how do you want me to use the resources you have entrusted to me?* This includes our wallets and purses — the cash, checkbooks, debit cards, credit cards, savings accounts, and all our other resources.

This practice is directly tied to the belief of stewardship: I believe everything I am and everything I own belong to God. Therein lies our dividing line. Do we perceive our money, our resources, to be God's or ours?

When Jesus redeems our souls, he can also redeem our financial management, debt, savings, investing, and giving. Our checkbooks, credit cards, savings accounts, stocks, bonds, and 401(k)s should all come under his authority and leadership.

As a pastor, I've counseled people on this topic for many years, and I can safely say that what keeps many Christians from giving isn't really their lack of desire, but rather an abundance of personal debt. All too often, debt comes not so much from medical bills from unforeseen illnesses or unavoidable tragedies as from intentional choices to accumulate stuff, which then places an almost unbearable burden for many years and prevents true freedom and blessing in giving to God and his kingdom.

In the Sermon on the Mount, Jesus teaches, "No one can serve two masters. Either you will hate the one and love the other, or you will be devoted to the one and despise the other. You cannot serve both God and money" (Matthew 6:24). Sadly, while many Christians today would say they love God and desire to serve him, their devotion must go to "serving" the payments demanded each month. Jesus' words are as accurate today as the day he first said them.

As we have stated with other key ideas, we give our resources with an eternal reason at the forefront — to fulfill God's purposes. Money will never save anyone's soul, but funds are needed to support ministries that reach people all over the world with the gospel of Christ. If we believe the only thing that will matter in heaven will be what we have done for Christ here on earth, then the vast majority of the money to go through our hands will not count for much — except what has been given to build Christ's kingdom.

KEY APPLICATION: What difference does this make in the way I live?

- We intentionally give a percentage of our financial resources to fuel the purposes of God and his kingdom.
- We intentionally make available the material resources God has entrusted to us (home, car, clothes, tools, food) to fulfill God's purposes in the lives of others.

Here is a valuable exercise. Take out your checkbook register and last month's credit card bill. Walk through the past thirty days and categorize your expenses. While potentially painful, I can promise it will benefit you in the days ahead. Ask yourself these questions:

1. What patterns or tendencies do I see?
2. What priorities are evident in my spending?
3. Where am I pleased with regard to my money management?
4. Where am I disappointed with my findings?
5. What changes should I consider making?

As you lay your finances before the Lord, ask, "Am I using the resources you've given me to accomplish your purposes?" If the answer is yes, thank God for his wisdom and provision for you, and continue to grow in giving. If the answer is no, then self-condemnation and regret are not the proper responses. The very good news is that God, who is faithful and just, will forgive you, and he is ready to help you direct your energy to the transformation of how you use your money.

So where do we start?

We go back to the heart. There's a decision to make. Whom will we serve? Ponder again these words of Jesus: "No one can serve two masters. Either you will hate the one and love the other, or you will be devoted to the one and despise the other. You cannot serve both God and money" (Matthew 6:24).

One man stated it well in his financial testimony: "I used to think I couldn't afford to give to God, but once I started, God blessed me so much I could no longer afford not to!"

If you don't already know this key kingdom principle, now is the perfect time to receive this truth: God has his own economy. He doesn't have to rely on the current condition of any nation to bless his people, and he isn't limited by anyone's actions. He can produce what he needs to provide, exactly when he desires to bring it forth. The people who have read the Scriptures on giving and decided to take God at his word also testify to the miracles he has shown when they put their trust in him and placed all their resources into the center of his economy. Remember, we are *in* the world, but not *of* it! Whether it takes us a few months or a few years of faithful obedience to get our financial house in order, God has the unique ability to multiply what his people offer him and bless what he is given access to.

Sharing My Faith

Pray also for me, that whenever I speak, words may be given me so that I will fearlessly make known the mystery of the gospel, for which I am an ambassador in chains. Pray that I may declare it fearlessly, as I should.

EPHESIANS 6:19–20

For a vast majority of Christians, particularly in our politically correct culture, talking with a nonbeliever about a relationship with Christ seems a daunting and intimidating task. Weather. Fashion. Sports. Current news. All good. Jesus? Not so much. Putting our message on the defense is a brilliant and clear strategy of Satan to keep people from hearing about salvation. But I'm confident that you quite likely became a Christian through someone who was willing to take a risk and reach out to share the good news of Jesus Christ with you. The apostle Paul writes:

How, then, can they call on the one they have not believed in? And how can they believe in the one of whom they have not heard? And how can they hear without someone preaching to them? And how can anyone preach unless they are sent? As it is written: "How beautiful are the feet of those who bring good news!" (Romans 10:14–15).

KEY QUESTION: How do I share my faith with those who don't know God?

The key belief of eternity—that there is a heaven and a hell and that Jesus will return to judge all people and to establish his eternal kingdom — is real. The destination of people for all time is fully based on them receiving forgiveness of their sins through Christ. He has provided the way of salvation, but people must embrace it individually for themselves. The gift is free, regardless of what they have done. No one is unsaveable. We, as his disciples, are here to let people know, by how we live our lives and by the words we speak, what we know about Jesus.

Year in and year out, decade after decade, statistics about how people come to faith in Jesus show a clear majority enter through a person who cares enough to share the gospel story. Relationships have always been, and still are, God's primary path for bringing people into his kingdom. God has one plan for saving the world: his people — us.

For more than two thousand years, Christianity has been one generation away from extinction, yet the plan keeps working. Faith moves forward. Do people still die without a relationship with Christ? Certainly, and unfortunately. Even still, our mission is simple: tell the message to all we can.

KEY IDEA: I share my faith with others to fulfill God's purposes.

After we receive Christ, we may each have different careers to make a living, but we all have the same job description. Paul tells us in 2 Corinthians 5:18 – 21:

> All this [our new life] is from God, who reconciled us to himself through Christ and gave us the ministry of reconciliation: that God was reconciling the world to himself in Christ, not counting people's sins against them. And he has committed to us the message of reconciliation. We are therefore Christ's ambassadors, as though God were making his appeal through us. We implore you on Christ's behalf: Be reconciled to God. God made him who had no sin to be sin for us, so that in him we might become the righteousness of God.

The job description? Ambassadors for Christ.

What does an ambassador do? Take God's message of reconciliation to the people of the world. Across the street or across the globe, we don't speak our message, but his.

How does this happen? "As though God were making his appeal through us." By his power, he will give us the opportunity and the words.

What is the appeal? "Be reconciled to God." God sent Jesus "to be sin for us"; to die so we wouldn't have to, so we can share in God's righteousness, because we have none of our own. The debt we could never pay has been paid in full! This is why the gospel is called the good news.

KEY APPLICATION: What difference does this make in the way I live?

We are never responsible to save, but only to share. Our goal is to bring revelation, not to broker a response. The end result is up to God. But we must learn to share our faith.

While there are many methods and resources for talking to people about Christ, here are two simple approaches to sharing your faith.

1. Share Your Story

As a Christian, you have a spiritual autobiography — a story to tell about how God saved you. It is your story, unique to you. The wonderful truth about your journey of faith is that no one can debate or argue with you about its validity. Jesus made himself real to you, and you believe it. So know your story, because you have one. Tell your story, because you can.

We've all heard the miraculous accounts of people who were delivered and set free from addiction and horrible circumstances. Maybe you were too. But here is the common denominator of all Jesus stories. We were all lost and destined for hell. He came, found us, and offered salvation. We received his gift and, therefore, were saved. Case closed. So no one's testimony is better or more interesting than anyone else's when the final scene is always the same — we are saved from death and set on the path of God's kingdom in and through a relationship with Christ.

In our "140 characters or less" Twitter culture, a precise, powerful testimony is best. Here's a simple flow for sharing your story:

1. In one minute or less, tell about your life before you came to Christ. Share your circumstances, the struggles, and the questions you had. What path were you on before Jesus?

2. In one minute or less, tell how you came to faith in Christ. Who shared with you? What circumstances surrounded the decision? How did you know this was the right choice?

3. In one minute or less, tell how Christ has changed you. What differences has he made? How has life changed after crossing the line of faith?

4. In one minute or less, tell what God is doing in your life right now. Even if you became a Christian twenty years ago, God is constantly working in you, so share what he is doing now, what he is showing you, and how you are growing.

You may find it helpful to take a half hour to write this out. Three to five sentences per point will usually suffice. Write it; learn it; share it.

2. Share Scriptures

Since God's Word has the plan of salvation, then share those verses. This particular method is known as the Roman Road.

1. **Why do we need salvation?**
   - Romans 3:10: "As it is written: 'There is no one righteous, not even one.'"
   - Romans 3:23: "All have sinned and fall short of the glory of God."

No one can get to God on his or her own. We all miss the mark of righteousness.

2. **What hope do we have?**
   • Romans 5:8: "God demonstrates his own love for us in this: While we were still sinners, Christ died for us."
   • Romans 6:23: "The wages of sin is death, but the gift of God is eternal life in Christ Jesus our Lord."

Out of his great love, God gave the gift of his Son to offer us eternal life.

3. **How can we be saved?**
   • Romans 10:9 – 10: "If you declare with your mouth, 'Jesus is Lord,' and believe in your heart that God raised him from the dead, you will be saved. For it is with your heart that you believe and are justified, and it is with your mouth that you profess your faith and are saved."
   • Romans 10:13: "Everyone who calls on the name of the Lord will be saved."

Believe in your heart and confess with your mouth that Jesus is Lord, and salvation is yours.

Paul's letter to the Romans contains other follow-up verses (e.g., 5:1; 8:1, 38 – 39), but these three simple steps are enough to lead someone to faith in Christ.

There are no magic words to save us; just a simple prayer from the heart will do. Here is a sample prayer of salvation:

Heavenly Father, I confess I am a sinner in need of a Savior. Please save me. Come into my life and change me. I want to spend eternity with you. Thank you for dying on the cross for me. Thank you for the new life you offer me now. In Jesus' name. Amen.

Regardless of how you choose to deliver the good news of the gospel, the most important element is that you are willing to share your faith. If you are willing and ready, God will bring the opportunities.

Can you recall the last time you shared Christ or at least told someone how important your faith is to you? When was the last time you invited someone to belief in Christ?

In the Christian walk, nothing is more exhilarating than letting people in on the difference God makes and how true life is found in Jesus. And then when we get to be a part of someone crossing the line of faith and taking hold of eternal life, it just doesn't get any better. When we are able to see someone point his or her life not only to God's kingdom but also to God's abundant life now, we fulfill the very reason God has us here.

We must always keep in mind how much God wants to save people. The criminal on the cross said to Jesus, "Remember me when you come into your kingdom" — to which Jesus miraculously responded with, "Today you will be with me in paradise" (Luke 23:42 – 43). This two-sentence exchange shows the deep longing in the heart of God to rescue people from sin and eternal death. We must simply join him in his work by sharing what he has done for us.

Closing Thoughts about Key Practices

I once heard a story about a man who attended an art show. He was amazed at a life-size statue of a lion. The details and scale were incredible. The man approached the sculptor, who was standing nearby, and asked, "How in the world were you able to fashion a lion so detailed out of a block of stone?" The artist smiled slyly and answered, "Well, it's easy, really. I simply chipped away everything that did not look like a lion."[26]

God is methodically and continually chipping away everything on us that does not look like his Son — the Lion of Judah. He is continually shaping and molding each of us into his image.

God's goal is that by the time we leave this world and enter his, we look as much like Christ as possible. Once we enter heaven, we receive our glorified bodies and are fully formed into his image. But as we've repeatedly stated, the reason to become like him now is so we can influence as many of our neighbors as possible to join us in his kingdom.

The ten "What Should We Do?" practices are some of the primary actions of Jesus — those movements of his we should mimic, those activities that keep us becoming like Jesus.

PART 3

Be Like Jesus
Who Am I Becoming?

My dear children, for whom I am again in the pains of childbirth until Christ is formed in you, how I wish I could be with you now ...

GALATIANS 4:19–20

A few years ago, we received a lemon tree as a gift from a family in our church. At the time, we didn't know much about how to care for a fruit tree. We read about how important the soil is to the health of the tree. We learned about the size of the pot in which the tree is planted and the proper way to prune the tree to make it more productive. We found out about the importance of water and the amount of sunlight, as well as the proper balance of both.

At last, the following spring, we saw our first lemon begin to grow. By the summer, we decided to make the transition from gardener to consumer. The sole lemon was green. *Maybe our friends gave us a lime tree*, we thought. We picked our lemon. I took a knife and cut our fruit in half. It turned out it was an unripened lemon picked too early by an inexperienced gardener. To our dismay, we had to throw our "bumper crop" into the trash. We learned, then and there, that even the timing of picking the fruit is crucial to consumption and enjoyment. Growing good fruit, while a labor of love, can also be a challenging task.

Jesus used the analogy of fruit to teach about the spiritual growth process. He said becoming like him is much the same as growing a crop.

> *"I am the true vine, and my Father is the gardener. He cuts off every branch in me that bears no fruit, while every branch that does bear fruit he prunes so that it will be even more fruitful. You are already clean because of the word I have spoken to you. Remain in me, as I also remain in you. No branch can bear fruit by itself; it must remain in the vine. Neither can you bear fruit unless you remain in me.*
>
> *"I am the vine; you are the branches. If you remain in me and I in you, you will bear much fruit; apart from me you can do nothing" (John 15:1 – 5).*

Jesus defines the roles involved in the garden of God's growth. He is the vine — the trunk of the tree or the primary stem from which grow both the roots inward and the fruit outward. Christians — those who believe in Jesus for salvation — are the branches, flowing and growing from the trunk or vine. God is the gardener who intervenes in the life flow of the branches to eventually produce and bear fruit. He plays the critical role in directing and overseeing the process.

As long as we stay connected to Jesus, we will "bear much fruit," but if we separate from "the vine," we will produce nothing. Not a little. Not some. But zero. These verses are a promise and an encouragement to stay close, grow, and produce tasty, attractive fruit for all. Not only will our lives be enriched, but, most importantly, the world will know the greatness of the Gardener.

How then do we "remain" in Christ?

The word means "to stay put; to continue in a specified condition; to endure." We stay attached in our relationship with God through Christ in seasons of flood or drought. We trust his hand and his process, and, in the end, we will bear much fruit. In John 15:9 – 10, Jesus says:

> "As the Father has loved me, so have I loved you. Now remain in my love. If you keep my commands, you will remain in my love, just as I have kept my Father's commands and remain in his love."

What are the Father's commands Jesus refers to here?

> " 'Love the Lord your God with all your heart and with all your soul and with all your strength and with all your mind'; and, 'Love your neighbor as yourself' " (Luke 10:27).

Our *vertical* relationship with God invites us to engage in the spiritual disciplines or practices, as we've previously discussed. These spiritual acts, inside biblical community, express and reinforce what we think and allow us to become like Jesus.

Jesus' second command has to do with the *horizontal* relationships in our lives — loving our neighbors. He did not make this difficult to understand or a mystery to figure out. It is quite simple: "My command is this: Love each other as I have loved you" (John 15:12).

These actions then express and reinforce the way we think like Jesus. The longer we remain in him, the more mature we become and the greater the fruit we produce. This process, in turn, brings growth to God's kingdom.

In Jesus' teaching, there is always an end goal. In John 15:11, Jesus says, "I have told you this so that my joy may be in you and that your joy may be complete." He desires for his joy to go into us. The vine feeds nutrients into the branch. The result? Our joy will be complete. In the New Testament, the word *complete* simply means "mature." So our joy is brought into maturity through remaining in him. Mature joy will be steadfast, secure, and solid in the face of any circumstance.

Joy will develop on the outside of our lives by first developing on the inside. It begins to bud on the branches and then it matures so others may enjoy the fruit. People like being around a joyful person, because their joy is contagious and uplifting. They "eat the fruit," so to speak, and find it sweet and delicious.

For people to know who you are and even *whose* you are, when they taste of this fruit from your life, they will conclude you are one of Jesus' disciples. In this world, where else can such a mature joy come from?

Take a look at this updated graphic as a visual reminder of this revolution of change:

Thinking like Jesus revolves the wheel to *acting* like Jesus, which then turns further to *being* like Jesus. Driven by the very presence of God, we are now almost at a complete revolution or rotation of change. This is a critical point of understanding in the process, because we are about to discuss outward life change in us that will be seen by others.

While Jesus speaks in John 15 about joy, ultimately he wants to see ten varieties of fruit grow on the branches of our lives. In the next ten chapters, we will focus on key virtues of who we are becoming in Christ: love, joy, peace, self-control, hope, patience, kindness/goodness, faithfulness, gentleness, and humility.*

As in previous chapters, we will explore three areas:

1. **KEY QUESTION:** What life question does this practice answer?

2. **KEY IDEA:** What are the essentials of engaging in this virtue?

3. **KEY APPLICATION:** What difference does this make in the way I live?

By the way, on the next go-around with our little lemon tree we were better-equipped gardeners. This time the lemons *remained* on the tree until harvesttime in the fall. The result? Thirteen amazingly tasty lemons for all to enjoy! God can and will do the same with our lives if we *remain* in his vine.

---

* Note that many of these key virtues are found in the list of the fruit of the Spirit in Galatians 5:22 – 23. We're using the term *patience* in this list (NIV, 1984 ed.) instead of *forbearance* (NIV, 2011 ed.), and we're linking two aspects of the fruit of the Spirit (kindness and goodness).

Love

This is love: not that we loved God, but that he loved us and sent his Son as an atoning sacrifice for our sins. Dear friends, since God so loved us, we also ought to love one another. No one has ever seen God; but if we love one another, God lives in us and his love is made complete in us.

1 JOHN 4:10–12

Love is a many-splendored thing.
Love is a rose, but you better not pick it.
Love is a battlefield.
Love is like a butterfly.
Love is all you need.
Love is a four-letter word.
Love is in the air.

Generations of poets and musicians have been attempting to define and capture the essence of love from every possible angle throughout time. Yet the poems and songs just keep coming. Why? Because love is such a powerful and vast force that we never seem to grow weary of hearing about it. Even still, we all struggle to adequately comprehend and express love on a daily basis.

Since God is the Creator, he is, therefore, the Creator of love as well. We must look to him to understand what this feeling truly means and how we can hold his love in our hearts while giving it away at the same time — just as Jesus showed us throughout his life and in his death.

KEY QUESTION: **What does it mean to sacrificially and unconditionally love others?**

There is likely not a more abused word, particularly in the English language, than the word *love*. We don't have a good method to rate the degree by which we are expressing the emotion. As a result, we love chocolate, and we love our children. The same? Of course not, but how does one differentiate the meaning? We love the latest song on the radio, and we love God. Again, while those two concepts come from entirely different places in our hearts, we use the same word to describe our feelings for each.

The New Testament writers understood this dilemma. They wanted to talk about this new brand of Christian love made possible through a real relationship with Jesus. There was just one problem — they couldn't find a word in the vocabulary of the Greek language to adequately describe the nature and quality of this new divine experience. So they took an existing word in the Greek language — *agape* — and infused it with new meaning to reflect this powerful concept of "God-centered love."

It's quite amazing and freeing to realize that human attempts to describe God's love for us resulted in a word that now has a meaning never before given.

KEY IDEA: **I am committed to loving God and loving others.**

The biblical word *love* has three unique and distinct characteristics.

Unconditional

Agape love is not dependent on love being given back. The old saying, "Love has to be a two-way street," doesn't apply here. While it is always great for feelings and actions to be reciprocated, there are no conditions or requirements for God's love to be experienced.

Many marriages today, and even friendships, are conditional

relationships — and many also are dependent on one of the two to be the instigator of the love or the expresser of love — as if to say, "Yes, I will love you, but you have to start, and then I will judge how well you love me before I decide how I will respond." Many relationships today seem to have more of a contractual character than a caring one. If any expectation or condition is not met, or at least perceived to *not* be met, love is withheld. It is right to question if this can truly be called love.

Simply put, agape love places no conditions, expectations, or stipulations on the other person for love to be expressed or displayed. It is, therefore, *unconditional.*

Sacrificial

Agape love places the other person first. Sacrificial love will take a risk by stepping out to show intent, regardless of the other's response. A person loving to this degree communicates, in effect, "I will lose some of who I am to love you. I will lay down my life. I will give up my rights. You are more important to me than I am to me!"

In Ephesians 5:25, this is the level to which Paul challenges husbands: "Husbands, love your wives, just as Christ loved the church and gave himself up for her."

This new "Jesus brand" of love gives itself up and takes risks for the welfare and care of others.

Forgiving

In our relationships with others, we often set each other up for failure by expecting perfection, which is impossible to attain. Agape love expresses, "You don't have to be perfect for me to love you and stay in a relationship with you. In fact, I expect you to be imperfect, so I will forgive. You don't have to earn my love. I factored in your mistakes and will allow for them." For the Christian, forgiveness is not isolated, individual dosings, but a lifestyle.

This is what God does for us daily. He is a God who forgives, and this is his assurance: "If we confess our sins, he is faithful and just and will forgive us our sins and purify us from all unrighteousness" (1 John 1:9).

Jesus invites us to do the same thing for others.

> Peter came to Jesus and asked, "Lord, how many times shall I forgive my brother or sister who sins against me? Up to seven times?"
>
> Jesus answered, "I tell you, not seven times, but seventy-seven times" (Matthew 18:21–22).

KEY APPLICATION: What difference does this make in the way I live?

Jesus' love in our hearts enables us to love those we could never love before.

In the Sermon on the Mount, recorded in Matthew's gospel, Jesus says:

> "You have heard that it was said, 'Love your neighbor and hate your enemy.' But I tell you, love your enemies and pray for those who persecute you, that you may be children of your Father in heaven" (Matthew 5:43–45).

Jesus is telling us that hatred is no longer an option for his followers. Regardless of how we are treated by anyone, the only choice is to love.

Jesus' love in our hearts enables us to love the unloved.

Matthew includes in his gospel Jesus' teaching about the gathering of the nations and the separating of the "sheep" from the "goats" that takes place when Jesus comes again:

> "Then the King will say to those on his right, 'Come, you who are blessed by my Father; take your inheritance, the kingdom

prepared for you since the creation of the world. For I was hungry and you gave me something to eat, I was thirsty and you gave me something to drink, I was a stranger and you invited me in, I needed clothes and you clothed me, I was sick and you looked after me, I was in prison and you came to visit me' " (Matthew 25:34–36).

Our world today has little time to spare for the homeless, poor, hungry, orphaned, diseased, elderly, and imprisoned. But Jesus clearly states that his followers will be about his business in those very places — to show love to the unloved.

Jesus' love in our hearts enables us to show the world what true love looks like.

Jesus lays out the ground rules for anyone who wants to be his follower:

> *"Anyone who loves their father or mother more than me is not worthy of me; anyone who loves their son or daughter more than me is not worthy of me. Whoever does not take up their cross and follow me is not worthy of me"* (Matthew 10:37–38).

To interpret this passage as Jesus urging us to not love our families or to shun them for his sake is to not take into account the context of the entire New Testament. Jesus is saying here that our love for him should be so strong and committed that all other loves can't possibly compare. The amazing thing about God is that when we do love him to this degree, our devotion and care for all people, including our families, will grow in ever-increasing measure.

The following story is an amazing display of God's love and a strong example of how radically a life can be changed by Christ.

Chris Carrier of Coral Gables, Florida, was ten years old when a man became so angry with Chris's father that he abducted Chris. The kidnapper burned him with cigarettes, stabbed him numerous times with an ice pick, shot him in the head, and then dumped him out to die in the Everglades. Miraculously, Chris survived and was found. His only lasting physical effect from the ordeal was losing sight in one eye. His attacker was never captured.

Carrier became a Christian and later served as a youth pastor at a church in Florida. One day, he received word that a man named David McAllister, a seventy-seven-year-old frail and blind ex-con living in a Miami Beach nursing home, had confessed to committing the crime all those years ago.

So Carrier headed to Miami. Did he take a gun? Did he plot revenge on the way there? After all, now the tables were turned. The old man was helpless, just as Chris had been when McAllister tortured and shot him, leaving him for dead. No. Revenge wasn't Chris's motive, as it had been his captor's. Carrier was going God's direction—toward forgiveness. And, amazingly, yes, even love.

Chris began visiting McAllister regularly and often read the Bible and prayed with him. Through these visits, Carrier eventually led McAllister to his Lord. Carrier said, "While many people can't understand how I could forgive David McAllister, from my point of view, I couldn't not forgive him. If I'd chosen to hate him all these years, or spent my life looking for revenge, then I wouldn't be the man I am today, the man my wife and children love, the man God has helped me to be."[27]

Each day as we live out our lives, Jesus loves us unconditionally and sacrificially, and he offers ongoing forgiveness. He asks us, his followers, to offer the same in our relationships. Why? This new breed of love allows us to be involved in healthy relationships and also to be free to express God's love to the world.

The apostle John sums it up: "We love because he first loved us" (1 John 4:19).

Joy

"I have told you this so that my joy may be in you and
that your joy may be complete."

JOHN 15:11

Remember Eeyore and Tigger in the *Winnie-the Pooh*-books? For
Eeyore, no matter what amazing circumstance came his way, doom
and gloom remained the focus. For Tigger, bouncing through life
without a care in the world, he never perceived anything to go
wrong. In our daily lives, it is easy to have the attitude of Eeyore
while wishing we could have the outlook of Tigger — two quite
extreme viewpoints of life.

The biblical brand of joy is not simply overcoming our inner
Eeyore, nor is it strolling through life in ignorant bliss; rather, it is
to be found in facing each day's ups and downs through the contentment Christ offers.

KEY QUESTION: What gives us true happiness and contentment in life?

The first order of business is to identify the difference between joy
and happiness. For many folks today, being happy is fully dependent on whether life is "all good." If someone asks, "Rate your life
right now on a scale of 1 to 10," often the number given is based
on the number of problems present. Happiness slides up and down
the scale, based on the perception of negative issues going on at
the time. Problems rise; happiness goes south. Troubles begin
to go away; the happy scale starts to climb. Joy, however, is not

dependent on circumstances, and, in fact, ironically, can become strongest when trouble comes. The psalmist reminds us of the reality of joy that comes when we rest in God's presence:

> You make known to me the path of life;
> you will fill me with joy in your presence,
> with eternal pleasures at your right hand (Psalm 16:11).

KEY IDEA: Despite my circumstances, I feel inner contentment and understand my purpose in life.

Joy has more to do with remaining in the presence of Jesus than with avoiding problems and struggles in our lives. Harkening back to John 15, we know that joy is always available to us when we remain in Christ, through whatever life brings. Let these statements guide you to see how true joy differs from mere happiness.

- Happiness is a state of mind, while joy is a mind-set.
- Happiness comes and goes, while joy can be constant.
- Happiness is dependent, while joy is independent.
- Happiness is conditional, while joy is unconditional.

The apostle Paul had learned the secret to the joy found in Jesus:

> I am not saying this because I am in need, for I have learned to be content whatever the circumstances. I know what it is to be in need, and I know what it is to have plenty. I have learned the secret of being content in any and every situation, whether well fed or hungry, whether living in plenty or in want. I can do all this through him who gives me strength (Philippians 4:11–13).

James drives home the definition of joy in the kingdom of God as having nothing to do with eliminating negative outward circumstances, but rather with embracing them as opportunities to strengthen faith and gain resolve:

Consider it pure joy, my brothers and sisters, whenever you face trials of many kinds, because you know that the testing of your faith produces perseverance. Let perseverance finish its work so that you may be mature and complete, not lacking anything (James 1:2–4).

Note the end result of choosing eternal joy — being mature and complete in Christ. Joy becomes the fuel for the believer on this road to maturity. Only Jesus can make our lives flourish in the midst of trouble. In him, joy is strengthened when life is challenging.

And finally, there is a source of deep joy available from an intimate place of serving Jesus. Take a look at his teaching in Luke 15:3 – 7:

Then Jesus told them this parable: "Suppose one of you has a hundred sheep and loses one of them. Doesn't he leave the ninety-nine in the open country and go after the lost sheep until he finds it? And when he finds it, he joyfully puts it on his shoulders and goes home. Then he calls his friends and neighbors together and says, 'Rejoice with me; I have found my lost sheep.' I tell you that in the same way there will be more rejoicing in heaven over one sinner who repents than over ninety-nine righteous persons who do not need to repent."

Joy comes when the lost are found! When we join Jesus in his work by sharing and seeing people come to him, we can be a part of the heavenly celebration right here and right now.

KEY APPLICATION: What difference does this make in the way I live?

The joy of Christ will replace or reduce stress.

Joy becomes a filter through which we view life. We're not talking about rose-colored glasses, but about actually having brand-new eyes! Joy can change our perspective and our perception of negative circumstances. We aren't simply in denial, sticking our head in the sand, but rather we choose to rise above the circumstances and adopt an eternal mind-set. Stress can come from many different factors today. We can worry and fret because we feel we're not in control. Joy is an ongoing reminder that God is in control — that he is in charge of the outcome. Joy comes from trusting the controller of all things.

The joy of Christ will become contagious through us.

As stated earlier, who doesn't want to hang out with a joyful person? Joy lifts others up, just as despair brings them down. If you choose joy on a regular basis, you will not only be a far more approachable and relatable person, but your attitude will rub off on others and make a big impact on all the environments you are in.

The joy of Christ will draw others to Christ.

An old saying goes, "You can catch more flies with honey than with vinegar." Another adage, often heard in sports settings, is, "Attitude is everything." A person exuding a joy and vigor about life is going to raise the question, "What makes him [her] so different?" When those around us can look at us and see that we choose to express joy, no matter whether life is good or bad at the moment — therein lies the strongest testimony we can offer, even without words.

Notice the path we have taken here — from an inward focus of ending personal stress to an internal transformation to an outward attraction of people to Christ. As joy grows in the heart and mind of the believer, it infiltrates the soul and then moves outward to impact others. Loving God and loving neighbor.

You've probably heard the word *countenance* before. It describes not only the look *on* your face but also the look *of* your face. The last entry in George Orwell's notebooks reads, "At 50, everyone has the face he deserves." Eventually your face forms to your attitude and the perspective you have on life from the inside.

When you see people who look angry, but then you realize they're not frowning — there's a bad countenance. But have you seen a bride on her wedding day? Or a mother seeing her newborn child for the first time? Usually a radiant countenance! How can you tell that something good, or bad, has happened to someone you're close to, even before they say a word? The countenance. As a Christian matures in the virtue of joy, the countenance becomes a gauge of growth.

In one of the Methodist Episcopal Church Missionary Society's yearly journals, this story appeared:

> A Hindu trader in India asked Pema, a native Christian, "What do you put on your face to make it shine so?" Pema answered, "I don't put anything on it." "Yes, you do," said the trader. "All you Christians do. I have seen it in Agra, and in Ahmedabad, and in Surat, and in Bombay." Pema laughed, and his happy face shone as he said, "I'll tell you what it is that makes my face shine. It is happiness in the heart. Jesus gives me joy."[28]

We all will have good and bad days. We will all experience life's ups and downs. But has life robbed you of your joy, or are you growing in this virtue? What does your face reflect to others? What does your attitude communicate about your faith? Happiness will be all too fleeting, but the joy of Jesus is available to your soul right now. When trials arise, choose to lean on him, and you will find his joy.

Peace

Do not be anxious about anything, but in every situation, by prayer and petition, with thanksgiving, present your requests to God. And the peace of God, which transcends all understanding, will guard your hearts and your minds in Christ Jesus.

PHILIPPIANS 4:6–7

Most people would define peace as a feeling, as a sensation in the soul. Yet, temporary substances such as alcohol and drugs can artificially create a "peaceful" or sedate mood in us. The problem comes when the feeling wears off, and we are left, once again, with the chaos of our souls.

As we saw with joy, biblical peace is not based on mere feelings or circumstances. In Scripture, the presence of peace is about right relationships with God and neighbor. We read about winning favor in the sight of God and man (Proverbs 3:4) or growing in favor with God and man (of Samuel, in 1 Samuel 2:26; of Jesus, in Luke 2:52). This indicates a peace with God (vertical) and others (horizontal). Relationships are complete, and respect is intact. One can sleep peacefully with no regrets, because matters of the heart are right.

KEY QUESTION: Where do I find strength to battle anxiety and fear?

If you were to ask people to give you a definition of peace in our culture, you would likely hear more about the absence of trouble than the presence of contentment. A biblical definition of peace refers not to the subtraction of anything, but rather to the addition of Jesus. Wherever Christ is present, peace is available.

This is how the apostle Paul summarized it in Romans 5:1 – 2:

> Since we have been justified through faith, we have peace with God through our Lord Jesus Christ, through whom we have gained access by faith into this grace in which we now stand.

KEY IDEA: I am free from anxiety because I have found peace with God, peace with others, and peace with myself.

I was on my way back from a day trip when my wife, Rozanne, called to tell me she was struggling with something in our relationship and that we needed to talk about it when I arrived home. I immediately became riddled with inner anxiety, because things were not right in our relationship. As soon as I returned home, we talked. All was resolved, and I was free from the anxiety. The same truth exists in my relationship with God, and even inwardly in regard to myself.

Jesus provides us the opportunity to have peace with God. His death on the cross satisfied God's wrath against sin. Yet we must choose to receive this peace offered in salvation. Again, Christ is present, so peace is available. Consider these words of Jesus:

> "Peace I leave with you; my peace I give you. I do not give to you as the world gives. Do not let your hearts be troubled and do not be afraid" (John 14:27).

> "I have told you these things, so that in me you may have peace. In this world you will have trouble. But take heart! I have overcome the world" (John 16:33).

In our relationships, Paul encourages us to choose peace whenever it is possible and in each situation, as much as we have responsibility for and control over: "If it is possible, as far as it depends on you, live at peace with everyone" (Romans 12:18).

We are sinners, as are those we are in relationship with, and so peace will evade us at times; it won't always be everyone's choice — even our own. Paul writes, "If it is possible, as far as it depends on you" — calling us to do all we can to live in peace, but to realize that even when others won't allow it, we can be at peace with ourselves and always be ready to offer peace to others. Why? Because Christ's peace is always available to us.

And even regarding enemies, God can work miracles. In Proverbs 16:7, Solomon writes, "When the LORD takes pleasure in anyone's way, he causes their enemies to make peace with them."

Peace is a choice Christ gives us access to out of our relationship with God, deep in our own soul, even in the noise of the world and in the face of those who may hate us. Where he is present, peace is present. These verses of Scripture remind us of this precious gift:

> In peace I will lie down and sleep,
>   for you alone, LORD,
>   make me dwell in safety (Psalm 4:8).

> The LORD gives strength to his people;
>   the LORD blesses his people with peace (Psalm 29:11).

> He will be called
>   Wonderful Counselor, Mighty God,
>   Everlasting Father, Prince of Peace (Isaiah 9:6).

KEY APPLICATION: What difference does this make in the way I live?

The peace of Christ brings an end to our soul's search for security.

When Christians are asked about their lives prior to salvation, we hear a consistent testimony that they were searching for internal peace because they hadn't had it in their lives. We also often hear people say after praying to receive Christ, "I just immediately felt a peace come over me." While this is a feeling, it is also the spiritual sensation of the depositing of the peace of Christ into the soul. This is no flippant, figurative statement, but a literal change of the heart. The presence of peace has come to live forever in a warring soul.

We must never forget that the nonbeliever cannot muster up the "peace of God, which transcends all understanding" (Philippians 4:7). A discussion about peace can open a large doorway to reaching those who do not know Christ. After all, who doesn't want peace? Every human throughout history has sought it. Regardless of what we may attempt to stuff into our souls, nothing will satisfy or accomplish what Christ can do. His brand of peace is the only one custom-built to fit our hearts. The book of Job contains these words: "Submit to God and be at peace with him; in this way prosperity will come to you" (Job 22:21).

The peace of Christ brings us a proper response to a hurting world.

If Jesus is The Answer, then we have the answer. If he is the Prince of Peace, we now hold him in our hearts. This allows us to speak peace into volatile situations, promote peace in the midst of madness, and carry peace into confusion. Much like a mother's calm presence can quiet the cries of a baby, we are empowered to usher the peace of Christ into any situation where we are present.

We should never gain the reputation for divisiveness and dysfunction, but rather live in such a way that we are known for harmony and unity. This atmosphere is found in the mind-set of Christ, and as his temples moving about in the world, we can be known as purveyors of peace. The psalmist writes, "Great peace have those who love your law, and nothing can make them stumble" (Psalm 119:165).

The peace of Christ brings us an invitation to the atmosphere of heaven.

As peace permeated life in the garden for Adam and Eve before the fall, peace will once again reign for those who spend eternity with God. Yet the peace of heaven is the same peace that fills the empty soul after receiving Christ as Lord. We can experience a taste of eternity when we make the choice to follow him. When troubles arise, choose his peace. When tempers flare, choose his peace. When egos clash, choose his peace. This new life transcends understanding because it is not of this world.

Peace, inexplicably, is most present when it shouldn't be present at all. It is most felt when life all around us is at war. Peace comes when it is most needed, like a warrior on the white horse coming over the hill just when things look grim. We can't describe it; we can't explain it; and we certainly can't manufacture it on our own.

The two verses with which this chapter begins were written by the apostle Paul when he was in prison for his faith. It is clear from reading Philippians that Paul was at complete peace with his life, even though he was facing difficult and even life-threatening circumstances. These verses come toward the end of the letter. He describes to the reader how to grab hold of a peace that "passes all understanding."

When it comes to difficult situations you can't immediately change or fix — broken, hurting relationships; illnesses or diseases; financial crises — go to God in prayer. Begin by rehearsing all the things you are thankful for — down to the smallest bit of beauty. Leave no stone unturned. Then lay your request before God. Just speak it out to him in complete honesty and clarity. Be specific. Offer to him the things beyond your control and ability to fix. As you engage in this spiritual practice of prayer, a peace beyond your comprehension will begin to bud on the end of your "branches."

In 1956, when Steve Saint was five years old, his father, Nate, flew with four other missionaries into the jungles of Ecuador to attempt to make contact with the most dangerous tribe known to man, the Waodani. After several months of exchanging gifts with the natives, the five men were speared repeatedly and hacked to death with machetes. Years later, Steve found out that a tribe member named Mincaye had delivered the blow that ultimately killed his father.

At the age of nine, Steve went to the Waodani territory for the first time to visit his aunt, who was a missionary there, and he visited every summer after that until her death. Her affection for the tribe was a major influence in Steve's life.

When he was fourteen, Steve and his sister, Kathy, decided to be baptized by a couple of Waodani tribe members in the water next to the beach where their father had been killed. Steve says he has never forgotten the pain and heartache of losing his dad. "But I can't imagine not loving Mincaye, a man who has adopted me as his own, and the other Waodani," he says. "What the Waodani meant for evil, God used for good," says Steve. "Given the chance to rewrite the story, I would not be willing to change it."[29]

This famous story of martyred missionaries and their families could have a much different ending — one filled with rage, bitterness, and hatred. But they pressed on despite horrible personal tragedy and saw God work miracles. Why? Because through forgiveness, the peace of Christ was chosen both as a response to the Waodani and as an eternal gift offered to the tribe. Once again, God used his people to bring peace and reach the unreachable.

When peace is our soul's foundation, the walls of our life will be stable. It will steady and maintain our thoughts, emotions, attitudes, and feelings. If we daily surrender to Christ when the storms of life threaten, his peace will keep us grounded and secure.

> The LORD bless you
>   and keep you;
> the LORD make his face shine on you
>   and be gracious to you;
> the LORD turn his face toward you
>   and give you peace (Numbers 6:24–26).

Self-Control

For the grace of God has appeared that offers salvation to all people. It teaches us to say "No" to ungodliness and worldly passions, and to live self-controlled, upright and godly lives in this present age, while we wait for the blessed hope—the appearing of the glory of our great God and Savior, Jesus Christ.

TITUS 2:11–13

The Bible often refers to our bodies, as well as the sin we create by our choices, as "flesh." We act out by the stimulation of the sin nature. Flesh wants to take care of itself and always be first, no matter the cost to anyone—including, ironically, one's self. The flesh causes damage, even to the point of self-destruction.

In our natural state, we are separated from God because of sin, essentially having no choice but to ultimately opt for self. While we can make some good choices and do some good deeds, we cannot keep our behavior consistent because of who we are. But as our key Scripture in Titus explains, the grace of God after salvation gives us a new choice. In every instance, we can now choose either our own way or God's way. We can say no anytime we choose by obeying God. Through Christ, we can practice self-control rather than out-of-control.

KEY QUESTION: How does God free me from addictions and sinful habits?

Jesus came to earth in the flesh so he could redeem the flesh. As we talk about self-control, we think of the taming and overthrowing of the flesh. The apostle Paul writes in Romans 8:3 – 4:

> *What the law was powerless to do because it was weakened by the flesh, God did by sending his own Son in the likeness of sinful flesh to be a sin offering. And so he condemned sin in the flesh, in order that the righteous requirement of the law might be fully met in us, who do not live according to the flesh but according to the Spirit.*

Essentially, there is a constant internal attack going on within us. Temptation, thoughts, and attitudes flow through us, wanting self to be on the throne and get its way. But there is another influence we must deal with as well:

> *Do not love the world or anything in the world. If anyone loves the world, love for the Father is not in them. For everything in the world—the lust of the flesh, the lust of the eyes, and the pride of life—comes not from the Father but from the world (1 John 2:15 – 16).*

The "world" is an external destructive influence on us too. These Scripture verses define the world as the lust from our hearts brought on from us wanting all we see, with pride as the ultimate root driving this systemic problem. From this reality, it is certainly no coincidence we find a big fat *I* smack in the middle of the word *pride.*

Whether the motivation to place self first is coming from our internal source, an external one, or even both, the flow of communication is the flesh telling our heart what to do. The flesh is bossing, sometimes even bullying, the heart around.

So, then, what do we do? How in the world can we counter this constant attack?

We return to John 15. The nutrients of Jesus flow from the vine into the branch, producing his fruit, not our own. We remain in him. We choose God over self. We crawl off the throne and onto the altar.

Sometimes the best way to fully understand a concept, such as self-control, is to redefine it, to look at it through a different lens.

KEY IDEA: I have the power through Christ to control myself.

Self-control as a fruit of the Spirit might be better understood as God-control. I control myself by giving control over to God. I surrender; the flesh gives up; God takes command. In fact, self-control is best achieved when harnessed to the practice of total surrender. How can anyone make strong headway at self-control without first surrendering to God's Spirit? How can someone totally surrender to God without developing self-control? The two work independently, yet together — each supporting and strengthening the other.

Paul draws a powerful analogy in his letter to the Ephesians: "Do not get drunk on wine, which leads to debauchery. Instead, be filled with the Spirit" (Ephesians 5:18).

The analogy is powerful. Negatively, when we *yield to the spirits*, eventually the power of alcohol takes control of our mind and bodies and typically leads to negative consequences. In the same way, as we *yield to the Spirit*, eventually the Spirit takes control of our lives and leads us to live out God's good will. Self-control is not about *trying hard* but about *yielding hard*.

Self-control is yielding to God's power to do the things we should — and to not do the things we shouldn't. The writer in Proverbs used the protective walls of a city as an analogy for self-control.

> Better a patient person than a warrior,
>   one with self-control than one who takes a city
>   (Proverbs 16:32).

Like a city whose walls are broken through
is a person who lacks self-control (Proverbs 25:28).

The distinct point here is that a person who is successful at self-control has won a greater victory than the warrior who conquered a city. It could also be said that one who maintains self-control keeps the boundaries of his life—the walls—safe and secure. This is an effective defensive device against the influence of outside forces.

KEY APPLICATION: What difference does this make in the way I live?

Pull up any news feed on any day from anywhere in the world —small town or metropolitan city—and you will read stories of people who lost their self-control. Murder, assault, abuse, drunkenness, sexual crimes, lies—and on and on the list goes. The common denominator in every crime that ends in a mug shot on the news is a person who gave in to the behavior in which he or she was tempted to engage. Granted, some decide they do not care at all about the consequences, but the vast majority will eventually regret they could not contain the emotion or feeling that fueled the fire that now consumes their lives. Imagine how many people sitting in jail cells today would say, "I'd give anything to be able to go back in time and control my actions."

Since none of us are exempt from temptation and sliding down a slippery slope to decadence, allowing self-control to be a growing and active virtue may just save our lives and the lives of those we love.

As we develop the virtue of self-control, our sin will decrease and our character will increase.

We will learn to say, along with John the Baptist, "He [Jesus] must become greater; I must become less" (John 3:30). As Christ takes over more and more territory in our heart, there is less of our flesh to interfere. As this transformation grows, sin's grip is loosened and God's qualities will show in ever-growing proportions.

As we develop the virtue of self-control, our relationship with God will mature at an accelerated rate.

Self-control is not only about the discipline to stop doing things that destroy us but also about the discipline to do the things that build us up. When we develop a healthy discipline to engage in the spiritual practices, we speed up our spiritual growth rate.

As we develop the virtue of self-control, our relationships with others will flourish and strengthen at an accelerated rate.

Our connection to others is empowered when we increase our own self-control. Disagreements, arguments, angry outbursts, misspoken words, and misguided emotions can be held at bay by controlling the tongue, which is a stronghold for self-control. You will become a better spouse, parent, family member, employee, church member, and so on if you work on yourself first to squelch your own flesh.

The late George Gallup Jr. was a good friend of mine who significantly helped me in the early journey of forming these thirty key ideas of the Christian life. In one of our several all-day sessions in Princeton, New Jersey, tucked away in the gun room of the historic Nassau Club, we were discussing this virtue of self-control.

I was pontificating proudly on how Christians just need to get their act together and be self-controlled. In George's always kind and gentle demeanor he stopped me and said, "Randy, you're not an alcoholic, are you?" Startled by the question, I said, "No, I'm not." He went on to say, "Well, I am. My father was also an alcoholic. When I took my first drink, something happened to me that likely didn't happen to you or many others. I was hooked and couldn't stop. Even as a Christian, I tried and tried and tried. I felt so defeated, and it was ruining my life. Then in a moment of quiet desperation, I heard Jesus whisper to me, 'George, if you never lick this, that is okay. I died for this struggle in your life, and I still love you deeply.'" He paused for a moment, reflecting on that tender encounter with the Savior, and then said, "From that very moment I haven't had a drink. It has been over thirty years."

At that meeting, we added the phrase "through Christ" to the key idea of self-control: "I have the power, *through Christ*, to control myself." Yielding to the love, grace, and presence of Christ in us is the only way we can be victorious. While not every Christian struggling with an addiction may experience the deliverance George did, the truth of Christ's commitment and deep love applies to all of us.

When Christ returns, our blessed hope having been made a reality, we will receive brand-new bodies that are free from the infection of sin. We will be alive eternally in heaven, where self no longer may rule, but only God. Sin and its devastating effects will be forever wiped away, along with the pain and tears created by temptation and sin.

Remaining in Christ today can allow us to overcome the world and the flesh. Self-control is possible when God is in control of us.

Hope

We have this hope as an anchor for the soul, firm and secure. It enters the inner sanctuary behind the curtain, where our forerunner, Jesus, has entered on our behalf.

HEBREWS 6:19–20

My mom had a debilitating fear of flying. To visit family that lived out of state, traveling by plane hadn't been an option for her. This all changed when our daughter was born in Texas. The only way Mom could see her new granddaughter was to fly from Cleveland to Dallas. She summoned all her courage and made the trip so she could hold Jennifer in her arms. The hope of seeing her new grandbaby allowed her to overcome her lack of faith in air travel, because she so desperately wanted to see the person at the other end of the journey.

Faith offers us the belief of eternity, but we live in, and are driven by, the hope that Jesus is at the other end of our journey.

KEY QUESTION: How do I deal with the hardships and struggles of life?

As we look closely at the virtue of hope, it is important to understand clearly what faith is. When we choose to exercise faith, we have no idea of what is coming ahead, but we believe God knows, and we believe he has the future in his control — no matter what. The author of Genesis describes how God worked in Abram's life, and how Abram responded:

The LORD had said to Abram, "Go from your country, your people and your father's household to the land I will show you.

> "I will make you into a great nation,
>   and I will bless you;
> I will make your name great,
>   and you will be a blessing.
> I will bless those who bless you,
>   and whoever curses you I will curse;
> and all peoples on earth
>   will be blessed through you."

So Abram went, as the LORD had told him (Genesis 12:1–4).

Abram expressed faith. He listened to God and acted on what he was told to do. The author of Hebrews provides this memorable definition of faith: "Faith is confidence in what we hope for and assurance about what we do not see" (Hebrews 11:1).

If faith begins the journey, then hope ends the journey. Hope is absolutely knowing where the road of faith will end; it is being confident of where the story concludes. Hope gives us the ability to endure the hardships and difficulties along the road of faith. We walk on in the hope of where the road leads.

KEY IDEA: I can cope with the hardships of life because of the hope I have in Jesus Christ.

To better understand biblical hope, we must determine what hope is *not*. If we live in the hope of our current circumstances — that they will either improve, or at least stay the same — this is a bad idea. We do not have such a guarantee. We can't sustain this type of hope.

Solomon wisely observed that we all get old — that hair and teeth fall out, things stop working — and eventually we and the people we love all die. Putting our hope in this life leads to colossal disappointments. Solomon called life with no reference to God "meaningless, a chasing after the wind" (Ecclesiastes 1:14).

But Christ offers something more; he provides what is true and viable — the hope of eternal life. In his letter to the Romans, Paul writes, "In this hope we were saved. But hope that is seen is no hope at all. Who hopes for what they already have? But if we hope for what we do not yet have, we wait for it patiently" (Romans 8:24 – 25).

As Christians, we must place our hope on the promise of what God has told us will come and the promise that Jesus is on the other side of this life. And the grand bonus is that we will be reunited with all those who have gone before us to heaven:

> Listen, I tell you a mystery: We will not all sleep, but we will all be changed—in a flash, in the twinkling of an eye, at the last trumpet. For the trumpet will sound, the dead will be raised imperishable, and we will be changed. For the perishable must clothe itself with the imperishable, and the mortal with immortality. When the perishable has been clothed with the imperishable, and the mortal with immortality, then the saying that is written will come true: "Death has been swallowed up in victory" (1 Corinthians 15:51 – 54).

Place your hope in what you will experience one day in God's new kingdom — eternal life in the very presence of God. This gives us the ability to endure the bumps and bruises along the road of life.

KEY APPLICATION: What difference does this make in the way I live?

Hope in Christ gives us a different place to look.

On a day-to-day basis, we have little choice but to stay focused on the physical world we live in. We have bills that need to be paid, problems that are waiting to be solved, and people who demand our attention. Hope of a future where God already resides and is in control, coupled with a home in his renovated and expanded garden for eternity, encourages us to keep looking forward and fix our eyes on him, not on the world. For the Christian, the best really is yet to come.

The author of Hebrews describes how hope gives us a different place to look: "Let us run with perseverance the race marked out for us, fixing our eyes on Jesus, the pioneer and perfecter of faith" (Hebrews 12:1 – 2).

Hope in Christ gives us a different way to think.

Our minds can be our greatest enemy or our strongest ally. How we think is what we will do and what we will become. Focusing on hope for today, our future, and into eternity creates a positive, optimistic, "glass half full" mind-set. In our mean-spirited, downward-spiraling culture, the person with an attitude of hope and uplifting thoughts will not only be a healthier person but also draw others to Christ by their very being.

The apostle Paul describes this different way to think: "Set your minds on things above, not on earthly things" (Colossians 3:2).

Hope in Christ gives us a different life to live.

Do you know someone who lives by the mantra, "If you thought today was bad, just wait until tomorrow"? Few people enjoy being around someone like this. Why? Because we all desperately want to enjoy life! We want to feel contentment and live in the hope of a good day and a brighter tomorrow. New life in Christ is not only a different way to live, but it's also the best way to live. Lifestyle choices and future direction fueled by the reality of divine expectation form a life based on nothing but hope.

In the words of the psalmist, "Be strong and take heart, all you who hope in the LORD" (Psalm 31:24).

Since the rise of Christianity and up to the current day, martyrs — those who die because of their faith in Christ — have been a strong segment of the population of believers. Why would someone choose to die rather than renounce Christ? Why would anyone suffer torture at the hands of evil dictators because of a belief they will not rescind? Why would people suffer from a lack of food, water, and medical care solely because they are Christians? What drives them to place their faith above anything else in life? The answer? Hope. What else could be the answer to these questions? For millions of Christians, the hope of Christ has driven them to survive mind-boggling odds and die peacefully under unspeakable circumstances. The longing to see their Savior on the other side fueled their hearts to endure to the end.

When you come to your final day here on earth, do you want to face it in terror, or do you want to confront it in hope? The great news is that you can face death with hope, but the even better news is that you don't have to wait until then. You can experience this hope right now. So jump on the plane of faith, in the sure knowledge of what and who awaits you on the other end. And in this life, you can echo the words of the psalmist in Psalm 33:20–22:

> We wait in hope for the LORD;
>   he is our help and our shield.
> In him our hearts rejoice,
>   for we trust in his holy name.
> May your unfailing love be with us, LORD,
>   even as we put our hope in you.

Patience

Whoever is patient has great understanding,
but one who is quick-tempered displays folly.
PROVERBS 14:29

Traffic. Deadlines. Annoying people. Standing in line. Being put on hold. Irritating people. Watching a file download. Being told a check is in the mail — again. Frustrating people. Bad ideas. Inept information. Incompetent people.

In this brief list of the areas in life where we tend to become impatient, did you notice the recurring characters? *People.* Ninety-nine percent of the time when we struggle with being patient, the words, actions, or attitudes of another person are the instigators. We can get rude with the one we love the most in life, but then also with a total stranger we will never see again. Impatience shows no favoritism in its victims.

Isn't it interesting that when we talk about patience today, we often refer to *im*patience? We say things like, "You are trying my patience." Or, "My patience is wearing thin." Or, "I'm just about out of patience with you." So much that has to do with our use of the word *patience* actually refers to our lack of it!

KEY QUESTION: How does God provide the help I need to deal with stress?

As many of us fly through life at breakneck speed, levels of patience seem to have dramatically changed — and not for the better.

Consider these scenarios as we think about how our inability to wait has impacted modern culture:

- writing e-mails versus handwritten (or typed) letters sent in the mail
- talking on cell phones versus landlines
- picking up food at drive-through windows versus sitting down for a well-prepared meal at home
- cooking in microwaves versus cooking on the stove
- downloading music on iTunes versus buying CDs
- streaming movies on a laptop versus renting DVDs
- using single-serve coffee pods versus multi-cup coffeepots

We find ourselves more and more often becoming frustrated because we have to wait five minutes to get what we want, whereas just a few years ago we might have had to wait five hours. We no longer want to wait — for anything. The old joke, "Lord, give me patience, and give it to me now!" describes us well. And so patience is a crucial virtue for a Christian. If you are known as a patient person, you will definitely stick out!

God provides help for our impatient souls in a number of ways.

1. By example. God's long-suffering in dealing with us provides an ongoing model of how we should respond to others and to difficult situations.

2. By empowerment. God's Spirit gives us the strength to see life through his eyes and not just view the urgency of the issue. His perspective, which he shares with us, can help us see the bigger picture.

3. By encouragement. Scripture is filled with inspirational and motivating words to slow us down and wait for God's timing and provision.

KEY IDEA: I am slow to anger and endure patiently under the unavoidable pressures of life.

In his letter to the Ephesians, the apostle Paul writes, "Be completely humble and gentle; be patient, bearing with one another in love" (Ephesians 4:2). In this verse, he places patience in the same company as humility, gentleness, and love. Doesn't it make sense that a humble, gentle, loving person would also be patient?

In Scripture, the Greek word *makrothymia* is often translated into English as "patience." This Greek word is a compound word — from *makro*, which means "long," and *thymia*, which means "anger." When you put the two words together, it carries the idea of "taking a long time to burn with anger."

A simple scenario might help here. Imagine being in an irritating situation and someone sticks a spiritual thermometer in your mouth to monitor how long it takes for your temperature to rise. A year later, you are in the same situation. Would the thermometer show that it takes longer to overheat than the previous year? If so, you are growing in patience, which means taking longer and longer to succumb to frustration and agitation.

Some Bible translations use the word *long-suffering* — a merging of two unique words to convey one thought. It's the idea that we will display restraint in situations where most would feel we have the right to criticize, complain about, defend against, or even attack another's behavior. But this virtue goes even deeper to the idea that we will reflect mercy toward the other person as a sign of our strength of character. We will not only refuse to defend ourselves; we will turn down any opportunity to offend the other person. We will "suffer long" before we will get upset.

The New Testament uses another compound word for patience — *hypomone*, from *hypo* ("under") and *mone* ("to remain"). This virtue encourages us to learn how "to remain under" the unavoidable pressures of life. It is often translated "perseverance." We can picture this pressure as a huge, heavy bag we carry on our back.

Certainly there are self-imposed pressures we should avoid altogether — overcommitting on our to-do lists, overextending our resources, putting ourselves in compromising situations. Then there are situations outside of our control — illnesses, a mate who goes through a dark and difficult season, a child who is born with a birth defect, accidents that take the life of a loved one.

In these unavoidable situations we might be able to relieve our pressure by doing the wrong thing — become addicted to prescription drugs to ease the pain, get a divorce, seek revenge. God encourages us "to remain under the pressure" of this situation because it is the right thing to do — stay in a relationship and keep working on it, forgive, and move on. God can also give us the resources and the motivation to slowly work toward change in difficult circumstances. The bottom line is while escape may seem like the *quickest* solution; God wants to offer the *best* solution for everyone inside the circumstances. If we are to be directed out, then he can be the one who says so.

Together these two words form our key idea: I am slow to anger [*makrothymia*] and endure patiently under [*hypomone*] the unavoidable pressures of life.

The author of Hebrews reminds us of how important it is to be people of patience:

> So do not throw away your confidence; it will be richly rewarded. You need to persevere so that when you have done the will of God, you will receive what he has promised (Hebrews 10:35–36).

How long does it take for you to lose patience? The interesting thing about answering this personal question is we typically view ourselves as more patient than we truly are. While we may certainly recognize relationships or settings where we struggle, the ones who will answer more accurately are those closest to us. Spouse. Children. Close friends. Coworkers. Fellow church members.

Why? Because we are more likely to be impatient with the

people we spend the most amount of time with. With strangers or people out in the community, we are typically able to hold our struggle inside. The darkness and the desire to explode are in our hearts; we just hold them in. However, the more time we spend with people, eventually the darkness just has to come out. But that isn't all — the more time we spend with people, the more they can irritate us and the more likely it is for them to be around when stress ensues. Often, due to our closest family's and friends' own issues, they know what buttons to push to heat us up. Of course, we do the same to them.

KEY APPLICATION: What difference does this make in the way I live?

The story is told of a man who in a conversation with God asks him, "How long is a million years to you?" God responds, "Like a minute." The man pauses and asks, "Then how much is a million dollars to you?" God tells him, "Like a penny." With a sly smile on his face, the man goes on: "Then, God, would you please give me a penny?" And God says, "Sure, in a minute."

This scenario is a comical spin on the truth that God is not bound by our time or circumstances — a truth that challenges our view that God should respond to us immediately versus when he chooses to respond to us according to his plan.

Ironically, in our Christian journey, the only way God can teach us patience and help us grow in this virtue is to give us circum stances where we must wait on him. All too often, we get tired of this process and start trying to make things happen.

Enduring in patience and trusting Christ help us see that whatever God unfolds will always be better than what we try to force to happen.

The apostle Peter reminds us of God's loving purposes: "The Lord is not slow in keeping his promise, as some understand slowness. Instead he is patient with you, not wanting anyone to perish, but everyone to come to repentance" (2 Peter 3:9).

At the root of impatience is mistrust. There are times when God wants us to wait, yet we doubt whether anyone will act on our behalf, so we choose to not wait. We take action on our own, outside of God's direction. In our impatience, we exhibit pride — thinking we can do things better on our own. If we trust someone, we will wait on them to act. If we truly trust God, we will wait on his timing as we commit to serving him while we wait.

The story of Abram and Sarai powerfully illustrates this principle. God promises them they will have a child. Ten years go by, and still no child. They think to themselves, *God must need our help. We should step in and get the ball rolling*:

> *Sarai, Abram's wife, had borne him no children. But she had an Egyptian slave named Hagar; so she said to Abram, "The LORD has kept me from having children. Go, sleep with my slave; perhaps I can build a family through her." Abram agreed to what Sarai said (Genesis 16:1 – 2).*

It doesn't take a licensed professional counselor to know this is a bad idea. The outcome is disastrous. Jumping ahead of God's plan is always a bad idea.

Enduring in patience and trusting Christ help us see that receiving something later is often a far better plan than receiving it now.

The faster we want a life event to occur, the more it usually means we aren't ready to handle the responsibility of it. TV commercials and credit card invitations prey on this fact of human nature. "We just *have* to have ..." is always a strong indicator that we should wait.

As we mature in Christ, we will see more clearly why his timing is perfect. He knows best when we need something; therefore, to trust his heart and hand to provide is far better than placing before him our selfish demands.

Someone once wisely said, "God never moves hastily, but when he does move, he usually moves swiftly."

Enduring in patience and trusting Christ help us see growth in our relationship with God—his ways, timing, and outcomes.

Waiting on God will always provide the strongest finish, bringing the ability to see circumstances as he sees them. This will, in turn, spill over into our interactions with our neighbors. Patience is a spiritual muscle that grows stronger as we quietly wait for God to answer. This is the way the author of Ecclesiastes sums it up: "The end of a matter is better than its beginning, and patience is better than pride" (Ecclesiastes 7:8).

Kindness/Goodness

Make sure that nobody pays back wrong for wrong, but always strive to do what is good for each other and for everyone else.

1 THESSALONIANS 5:15

Our key Scripture verse commands us to strive, not to get even, but rather to do the right thing, no matter what. The Christian's response should be the *action* of Jesus, not the *reaction* of the world.

A popular bumper sticker a few years back read, "Commit a random act of kindness today." This is an obvious counter-strategy to "random acts of violence." Often when a person decides to engage in kindness toward someone, they will plan out a list of "good things" to do. But even a few intentional acts do not a kind person make. Why? Too often these are just short-lived efforts to influence or woo another, for the benefit of the person doing the deed.

A man was walking up to the large glass doors of a corporate building at the same time a female executive approached. He opened the door wide and stepped back, smiling as he motioned for her to walk in ahead of him. She stopped, glared at him, and blurted out, "You're only opening the door for me because I'm a woman, aren't you?" The man smiled and calmly replied, "No, ma'am. I'm opening the door for you because I am a gentleman."

The man was letting her know his actions were determined not by *her gender* but by *his nature.* Such is the biblical brand of kindness and goodness. It acts as it is, no matter the circumstance. Not random acts, but redeemed pro-activity.

KEY QUESTION: What does it mean to do the right thing in my relationships?

It's likely you know someone who will occasionally do a good deed for you, but you wouldn't describe this person as a kind person. But you can also think of someone who consistently exudes a good nature because it is who this person is. Think about the difference in saying, "What a nice thing for you to do" versus "You are such a kind person." Biblical kindness/goodness is the outcome of an intentional Christian lifestyle. A person whose nature is good will be kind. A kind person will be a good person.

While kindness has a relatively clear connotation in our culture, goodness can be left open to various interpretations and to one's own standards. Consider Jesus' words to a rich man who asked him a question about what good thing the man needed to do to gain eternal life: "'Why do you ask me about what is good?' Jesus replied. 'There is only One who is good. If you want to enter life, keep the commandments'" (Matthew 19:17).

For our purposes here, let's define goodness in terms of our consistently reflecting the character of God in our motives and actions. As goodness gains ground in the maturity of a believer, those around this person will notice fruit that draws them to God, the One who is truly good. This fruit will exude from the person's spirit, causing others to say, "There's just something different about this person. She's changed in dramatic ways."

Jesus was good throughout his entire being. Goodness ruled his every motive, thought, word, and action. In and through his goodness, he continually exhibited kindness through his miracles, healing, and teaching, whether his interactions were one-on-one or with the masses. The goodness was driven by his love for God; his kindness was driven by his love for neighbor. The two work together; they are intertwined.

In every situation and circumstance, Jesus is God; therefore, Jesus is good. For us to be good by nature and to exhibit his kindness, we must love and live from his Spirit. When Jesus taught about good trees and good fruit and about bad trees and bad fruit, he said, "A good man brings good things out of the good stored up in his heart, and an evil man brings evil things out of the evil stored up in his heart. For the mouth speaks what the heart is full of" (Luke 6:45).

KEY IDEA: I choose to be kind and good in my relationships with others.

It is helpful to study the words for "kind" and "good" in the Bible's original languages to see the full force of meaning in color rather than simply in black-and-white.

Hesed is the primary Old Testament Hebrew word for "kindness." My Hebrew professor in seminary wanted to show us the depth of beauty in studying the Bible from the original language. To illustrate, he taught us that *hesed* comes from the same root word in Hebrew used for a *stork*. The stork is the only bird that will adopt a stray bird not of her kind and will love and care for it as family. So, too, God has adopted us and shows us the same lovingkindness one would show to a biological child. *Hesed* is loyal love over the long haul. As Christians, we are called to mimic the character of God from the inside out.

Kalos is a Greek word translated as "good" in the New Testament. It refers to an outward, aesthetic beauty. When we gaze at the Grand Canyon, an exotic flower, or a magnificent sunrise and whisper, "This is good," that's *kalos*.

And while our Creator God invites us to soak up and enjoy beauty, *kalos* isn't the word used when he calls us, through the teaching of the apostle Paul, to be kind and good. In the famous list of the fruit of the Spirit in Galatians 5:22 – 23, Paul uses two other Greek words. *Chrestos* (translated as "kindness") and *agathos* (translated as "goodness") refer to outward acts toward others that are first generated from an inner moral sense of what is right and best. We do what we do for others because inwardly in our hearts we have decided this is the right thing to do for the benefit of that person.

Imagine walking into someone's home and seeing a bowl of enticing fruit on the dining room table. You grab a piece, bite into it, and promptly break a tooth! What happened? Artificial fruit produced in a factory looks amazingly real by scale, color, and detail — but it is, by nature, fake food. Fake fruit has only one purpose: to be on display — great to look at, but of no real personal value.

There are times when an ulterior motive makes an act of kindness artificial. We can do something to look nice, to look good, and even to give the appearance of being harmless, but we may do it with the wrong motive. We give someone a public compliment, but we're doing it just so we can get something we want. We buy someone a gift, but our real goal is to get the person to do something for us — usually something far more valuable than the item we gave. Honest appearances can disguise highly dishonest motives. Some fruit is fake. Some acts only appear to be kind, but they are not good.

The book of Proverbs warns of those who sound good but who are out to do harm:

> Like a coating of silver dross on earthenware
>   are fervent lips with an evil heart.
> Enemies disguise themselves with their lips,
>   but in their hearts they harbor deceit.
> Though their speech is charming, do not believe them,
>   for seven abominations fill their hearts
>   (Proverbs 26:23–25).

Any artificial fruit will never taste good to the soul. If we bite into it, we will regret it. Real fruit, however, can look great and taste great for nourishment and sustenance.

KEY APPLICATION: **What difference does this make in the way I live?**

Out of a pure heart to do the right thing for others, we seek to build others up.

Every morning, we ask God to give us opportunities to take the good he is depositing in our hearts and give it away to others. We approach every day on the lookout to encourage others. In every conversation and encounter, we try to do something or say something kind, because it builds people up. In Christ, we have a bank account with unlimited kindness, and we seek to bless others by giving it away.

Out of a pure heart to do the right thing for others, we do not pay back wrong for wrong.

Just because someone has done us wrong, we don't see it as a license to return the wrong. Many people feel justified in being nasty to people who have first been nasty to them. Not so with God. Jesus tells us to "turn to them the other cheek" (Matthew 5:39). In Jesus' day, when someone slapped someone on the cheek, it was not meant to hurt them physically but to insult them publicly. When this happens to a growing Christian, Jesus urges them to take this insult into the heart to consider their response. The darkness that used to reside in the heart is no longer there. Little by little it has been cut out. The heart sends a message to the mouth to say, "I don't have an insult to return to you, so I guess it is your turn again."

In this chapter's key verse, Paul tells us to "make sure that nobody pays back wrong for wrong" (1 Thessalonians 5:15). The Greek word for "wrong" is *kaka*. Isn't that an appropriate word for it? We know "*kaka* happens" in a fallen world, but we refuse to return it to others. Rather, we seek to return good for evil, knowing it will drive that person either to madness or to repentance. Paul writes in Romans 12:19–21:

Do not take revenge, my dear friends, but leave room for God's wrath, for it is written: "It is mine to avenge; I will repay," says the Lord. On the contrary:

> *"If your enemy is hungry, feed him;*
> *if he is thirsty, give him something to drink.*
> *In doing this, you will heap burning coals on his head."*

Do not be overcome by evil, but overcome evil with good.

Out of a pure heart to do the right thing for others, we do the hard thing out of love.

We know there are times when the morally right thing to do in a relationship, where we've earned the right to do so, is to confront a friend or family member because it is best for them. We do so prayerfully, gently, and thoughtfully, as Scripture reminds us:

> *Brothers and sisters, if someone is caught in a sin, you who live by the Spirit should restore that person gently (Galatians 6:1).*

> *Speaking the truth in love, we will grow to become in every respect the mature body of him who is the head, that is, Christ (Ephesians 4:15).*

> *Faithful are the wounds of a friend,*
> *But deceitful are the kisses of an enemy*
> *(Proverbs 27:6 NASB).*

When a friend is clearly taking a wrong path, who will love them enough to warn them? You! They may reject you today, but eventually you will be the one over the long haul who proved to be a friend. You are willing to lose today because in your heart you know it is the right thing to do.

Christ modeled a life of complete kindness and goodness toward others. When others bit into the fruit of Jesus' life, they found it always ripe, sweet, nourishing, and refreshing. They experienced the truth of the psalmist's testimony in Psalm 34:8:

> *Taste and see that the LORD is good;*
> *blessed is the one who takes refuge in him.*

As Christ has his way in our lives, the nutrients of the Christ vine will make their way into our mouths, our hands, and our feet and produce amazingly delicious fruit for others to enjoy. The look on their faces after they taste the fruit from our trees will bring smiles to our faces and a keen awareness that God is working out his good plan for us. Paul's prayer for the Thessalonians is a prayer for us as well:

We constantly pray for you, that our God may make you worthy of his calling, and that by his power he may bring to fruition your every desire for goodness and your every deed prompted by faith (2 Thessalonians 1:11).

Faithfulness

Let love and faithfulness never leave you;
bind them around your neck,
write them on the tablet of your heart.
Then you will win favor and a good name
in the sight of God and man.

PROVERBS 3:3–4

Most people would connect the virtue of faithfulness to the context of a marriage covenant, whether in the positive sense of being faithful or in the negative sense of being unfaithful. When two people express a commitment to each other that will span a lifetime, marriage can certainly be one of the best cultural pictures of this virtue. Sadly, though, for far too many couples, marriage can become the worst picture. Some spouses decide faithfulness has a limit and is no longer worth the effort. Then there are people like Robertson McQuilken, who embrace and embody the biblical definition of faithfulness.

McQuilken resigned as president of Columbia Bible College in 1990, realizing he needed to focus his attention on caring for his wife, Muriel, who suffered from early onset Alzheimer's disease. Here is an excerpt from a letter he wrote to the college constituency:

> Recently it has become apparent that Muriel is contented most of the time she is with me and almost none of the time I am away from her. It is not just "discontent." She is filled with fear — even terror — that she has lost me and always goes in search of me

when I leave home. So it is clear to me that she needs me now, full-time. The decision was made, in a way, forty-two years ago when I promised to care for Muriel "in sickness and in health ... till death do us part." So, as I told the students and faculty, as a man of my word, integrity has something to do with it. But so does fairness. She has cared for me fully and sacrificially all these years; if I cared for her for the next forty years I would not be out of her debt.

Duty, however, can be grim and stoic. But there is more: I love Muriel. She is a delight to me — her childlike dependence and confidence in me, her warm love, occasional flashes of that wit I used to relish so, her happy spirit and tough resilience in the face of her continual distressing frustration. I don't have to care for her. I get to! It is a high honor to care for so wonderful a person.[30]

Robertson McQuilken is a modern-day inspiration and an example of faithfulness that is motivated by a deep love and commitment to both Christ and his wife.

KEY QUESTION: Why is it important to be loyal and committed to others?

The ultimate example of faithfulness in the Old Testament is seen in God's relationship with the nation of Israel. No matter what the people did, how quickly they turned on him, or how long they disobeyed him, God remained vigilant and available. The psalmist declares this truth:

> The LORD has made his salvation known
>   and revealed his righteousness to the nations.
> He has remembered his love
>   and his faithfulness to Israel;
> all the ends of the earth have seen
>   the salvation of our God (Psalm 98:2–3).

In the New Testament, Jesus showed a striking faithfulness both to the Father and to us, accomplishing the redemption of mankind on the cross. He stayed true to who he was and to his calling to bring us back to God.

As we've stated for all the virtues, the true path of biblical faithfulness is not an isolated event or events, but a way of life. We need not simply do faithful things; we must be faithful people. Then the result will be faith-filled actions flowing from a faithful heart.

KEY IDEA: I have established a good name with God and others based on my loyalty to those relationships.

Luke's gospel contains this description of Jesus during his growth into manhood: "Jesus grew in wisdom and stature, and in favor with God and man" (Luke 2:52).

This is a crucial and pivotal sentence in Scripture, because it is the bridge between Jesus' boyhood and the beginning of fulfilling his divine calling as a young man. The Bible establishes Jesus' birth and presence on the earth through fact and historical reference, and then cuts to the chase, jumping straight to the beginning of Jesus' ministry and path to the cross. This is one of those key verses where so much is communicated in very few words.

- Jesus grew in *wisdom*. His knowledge and character were developing beyond his years.

- Jesus grew in *stature*. He grew up as a normal, healthy boy into a full-grown adult.

- Jesus grew in *favor with God*. He remained faithful to God throughout boyhood, adolescence, and early manhood.

- Jesus grew in *favor with man*. His faithfulness to God and increasing wisdom resulted in right relationships and a good name as a man of honor and integrity.

Our key idea and this verse encourage us on every possible level to understand that faithfulness and commitment to God will result in the best possible life we can live — never exempt from problems or trials, but consistently walking on the right path toward the character and qualities of our Father.

In the parable of the bags of gold, Jesus describes the reward for those who have been faithful with God's resources on earth: "His master replied, 'Well done, good and faithful servant! You have been faithful with a few things; I will put you in charge of many things. Come and share your master's happiness!'" (Matthew 25:21). Putting God's blessings to the best use as a way of expressing our love and commitment to him brings continued blessing — the consequence of faithfulness.

KEY APPLICATION: What difference does this make in the way I live?

The virtue of faithfulness will translate in two ways in our lives.

- **We will be faithful to God.** No matter who follows or falls away, we remain in God. We do not wait for others to step out in faith; we lead. We don't shrink back when God's commands are not politically correct to obey; we simply do it. When God looks at us, he sees committed followers. Our best motivation for this choice is our love for him and the knowledge that he always does what is best for us. Our own faithfulness is motivated and led by his deep commitment to our lives and eternity. Our commitment to faithfulness leads us to love God more and more.

  Christians are not called to be successful as the world defines success. We are called to be faithful to God in what he calls us to do. We faithfully act in faith toward God and leave the results to him. If I die with five billion dollars in the bank but do not know and have not been faithful to God, then I have failed. If I end up broke but know God and have been faithful to his call on my life in the strength his Spirit provides, I have been truly successful. A genuine Christian embraces this axiom and escapes many of the temptations that can lead us astray.

• **We will be faithful to others.** The second way this virtue is seen is in our horizontal relationships. The people around us come to know we are loyal, trustworthy, and consistent. We can be counted on. We will be available. We will listen intently. We will answer the call for help. We model God's faithfulness by our lives freely given to others. Our commitment to faithfulness leads us to love our neighbors more and more.

The online Urban Dictionary is a publication for new slang and buzzwords added to our vocabulary on a regular basis. One word on its site is *sticktoittiveness*, defined as "the ability to persevere and endure to the point of overcoming a particularly difficult obstacle."[31] Faithfulness is the ongoing act of sticktoittiveness in both relationships and circumstances.

It is important to understand that being faithful to God is never about meeting a requirement to keep our relationship with him, but rather it's about responding to God out of love and devotion for what Christ has done for us. We choose to remain in him, not out of obligation, but out of desire.

Faithfulness must be a priority, no matter who is watching us. When we are alone or in a crowd, we're faithful; in good times or bad, we're faithful; when confident or in doubt, we're faithful. If we truly want to influence people for Christ, then being faithful has to be more than a desirable quality; it must become a lifestyle.

Gentleness

Let your gentleness be evident to all.
The Lord is near.

PHILIPPIANS 4:5

In a nationwide study conducted by the Gallup organization on the thirty key ideas in this book, gentleness came in dead last. The quality of gentleness appears to be a rare and evasive one in our culture — no matter whether someone is a Christian or a non-Christian. Both groups admitted this characteristic was severely lacking, making it the number one nemesis inside their own heart.[32]

"Are you known as someone who raises their voice?" is the question that tanked them. Of all thirty statements, this one gave the most people the biggest problem. While Christians scored slightly higher in exhibiting gentleness than non-Christians, both readily admitted their intense struggle to express this quality.

KEY QUESTION: How do I demonstrate thoughtfulness and consideration toward others?

What is it about this particular virtue that gives us fits? As a society, and even in the church, why are we so uptight? Tense? Stressed out? Why is gentleness such a stranger to so many? A greater question to ask is this: If Christ is present in our lives, why aren't Christians markedly gentler than those who do not follow the gentle Healer?

As we open the Bible, we find insight into how we can become more like Jesus for the sake of those God has placed in our lives.

KEY IDEA: I am thoughtful, considerate, and calm in my dealings with others.

When Paul used the word *gentleness* in our key verse in Philippians 4:5, he selected the Greek word *epieikeia*, which connotes a thoughtful, considerate, and decent outlook. Rather than hotly demanding their rights, whatever the cost to others, those with this trait seek peace in a calm way.[33]

When Paul picked the word *gentleness* to depict an aspect of the fruit of the Spirit in Galatians 5:22, he selected the Greek word *prautes*. In Paul's day, this word was linked to the medical world and carried the idea of a "mild medication." We might say a gentle person is someone who is "easy on your stomach." This is a perfect word picture, isn't it? Think of a churning stomach, that almost nauseating feeling you get when you know you're going to encounter a prideful person who, while they may be right much of the time, dispenses doses of medicine that are too rough on you.

This word was also used in reference to tamed animals. Think about a horse. These animals weigh an average of a thousand pounds and have the potential to seriously injure or even kill human beings. Yet we can walk up to the vast majority of horses, pet them, ride them, and deem them as gentle. Is this a reflection of their power and strength? No. It is an indication of their nature — what they are like after being trained. Gentleness for a horse is a choice to allow his power and strength to be controlled. A gentle person is not a weak person, but rather someone who is strong, secure, and mature. They use their strength to face real giants and challenges in their lives but choose not to run roughshod over others.

Together these two Greek words, *epieikeia* and *prautes*, reflect the opposite of an angry harshness that grows out of personal

pride and a dominating selfishness.[34] Christ wants us to become
gentle for the sake of others.

KEY APPLICATION: What difference does this make in the way I live?

In the book of Proverbs, Solomon reminds us of the importance of
exhibiting gentleness in the way we treat others:

> *A gentle answer turns away wrath,*
>   *but a harsh word stirs up anger (Proverbs 15:1).*

- **We are thoughtful.** We take the time to assess a situation and
  get the whole story. We don't move through life like a bull in
  a china shop, but we care about people along the way. We try
  not to take things for granted. We find ourselves often asking
  the question, "How are you doing?" We want to be known for
  doing little things behind the scenes to encourage people.

- **We are considerate.** When we're in a position to make a
  decision, we consider the impact on others. We seek their
  input before we pull the trigger. We do our best to put
  ourselves in the other person's shoes. We study the people
  God has put in our lives to discover what energizes them,
  what sets them off, and what buttons not to push.

- **We are calm.** While we will have moments when passion and
  aggression are right and necessary, there is great strength in
  our convictions when we hold to them in quiet confidence.
  A calm parent is more effective than a raging lunatic! It
  unnerves children when we look them in the eye and speak
  calmly. When approached by a rough, heated individual, we
  resist the temptation to meet fire with fire and walk away if
  necessary to defuse the situation. Because it's easy to become
  harsh, impatient, and arrogant when we're too busy and
  stressed, we seek to live lives where we take time to breathe,
  smell the roses, and pace ourselves.

Think about this self-evaluation question regarding the virtue of gentleness: If you had plans with someone for Sunday evening, would they be dreading the time with you or excited about the visit? Would they be expecting you to be calm or abrasive? Would they anticipate you to be thoughtful and attentive or self-focused and distracted? Would they leave the time with you feeling encouraged or discouraged? Worn-out or refreshed?

The problem with this scenario, though, is that self-evaluation is deceptive. We cannot fully see and understand our lack of gentleness. What we do is normative; we are the benchmark. Our lack of gentleness doesn't bother us too much. Our outburst is justified in our minds because of the rudeness and stupidity of insensitive and ignorant people. Someone has to fix the mess they are making. Our lack of gentleness is not a problem but a solution. Or at least this is how we tend to see it.

If we want to know the true measure of our gentleness, we have to ask others. Gentleness is a fruit; it is external, and everyone will be eating our fruit when they spend time with us. If it is sour, they will know; if it is sweet, they will know. The problem is that if we truly lack in the virtue of gentleness, these folks will be afraid to tell us the truth, lest we attack them. We have to find someone who is secure enough in Christ to tell us the truth in love.

Years ago, we owned a wonderful little home on a cozy street lined with pecan trees in suburban Texas. I was trying my best to be a good homeowner on a very small budget. In Texas, it's almost a necessity to have an in-ground sprinkler system, which we did not have. I couldn't afford to hire a company to install one, so a member of my staff, who had installed such a system (or at least led me to believe he had), came over to help me get the job done.

As you might suspect, we didn't do it correctly. Little did I know the implications of this mistake. At five o'clock each morning, the sprinklers would go off in the backyard and shoot streams of water over my fence onto my neighbor's wood-shingled roof. Not a good thing over time. To make matters worse, my neighbor was a retired Englishman who did everything with meticulous excellence — made possible with unlimited time, quite a lot of money, and a perfectionistic personality.

One sunny afternoon, I was working out in the yard, and my neighbor called out to me. I started making neighborly chitchat with him. He quickly cut me off and proceeded to tell me about the water that was being sprayed onto his roof. If he had just stopped there! But he didn't. He laid into me big-time. Let's just say there were expletives and threats of lawsuits. I was devastated. I was sick to my stomach. His brand of medication didn't settle well with me. I apologized and fixed the problem, but our relationship was injured. I wanted to confront him, but, frankly, he scared me.

About a month later, he knocked on our door. I was at work, but Rozanne, my wife, answered the door. Some branches from one of the trees on my property were hanging over his roof. He asked Rozanne if I would cut it down — and he was willing to help pay for it. Rozanne, a secure person who wasn't afraid of my neighbor (at least not yet), proceeded to speak a few words of calm truth into his life that I doubt he'd heard much before.

She said, "You know, I'm sure Randy would be more than happy to take this tree down, but you really hurt his feelings a few weeks ago." She proceeded to recap the brutal conversation from my perspective. When she finished, he expressed that he hadn't realized that his lack of gentleness toward me had crushed me the way it did. Something got through to him, because he said to my wife, "You know, I am just a grumpy old man. You tell him to come see me when he gets home."

In fear and trepidation, I did. My neighbor apologized to me. I cut down the tree at my expense, and we became the best of friends.

My neighbor's lack of gentleness would have continued as a pattern had it not been for the loving, constructive confrontation of my wife. Through the process, I also learned how to be a better neighbor. Before I start doing home projects, I check with my neighbors to make sure I'm not injuring their investment and stirring up their anger.

What lesson did I learn? That I don't like living around people who give me an upset stomach. When I swallow the medicine they give out, it might be good for me, but it's just too harsh on my system. As a Christ follower, I certainly don't want to be a "pill" to the people God put in my life to love. Fortunately, I have a loving, gentle wife who will tell me the truth in love. As I've asked for feedback and learned more about how to be gentle, little by little I am becoming more like Christ and people are not afraid to come to me.

Jesus extends the invitation: "Come to me, all you who are weary and burdened, and I will give you rest. Take my yoke upon you and learn from me, for I am gentle and humble in heart, and you will find rest for your souls. For my yoke is easy and my burden is light" (Matthew 11:28 – 30). I want to be able to say this to the people God has placed in my life. How about you? With Christ in us, we can be gentle! I know I'm not quite ready yet, but soon I want to openly invite the Gallup team to pay me a visit and ask me — better yet, ask my family and neighbors — "How is Randy doing with the fruit of gentleness?"

Humility

Do nothing out of selfish ambition or vain conceit. Rather, in humility value others above yourselves, not looking to your own interests but each of you to the interests of the others.

PHILIPPIANS 2:3–4

In 1884, King Humbert of Italy was awakened at midnight by a messenger informing him that an epidemic of cholera had broken out in Naples. Though the king was scheduled to be in Monza the next day for a magnificent reception, he telegraphed his hosts: "Banquet at Monza; cholera at Naples; I am going to Naples. If you don't see me again, good-bye."

John Stoddard tells what happened from there:

On reaching Naples, King Humbert found only the common people at the station to receive him. The rich, the aristocracy, and even most of the officials had fled. The king, however, did not care for that. It was the people he had come to save. For weeks, he worked incessantly to check the plague and to relieve the sufferers; he entered the hospitals, took the hands of the sick and dying into his own, and by his example shamed others into duty. After a week, one of his ministers said to him, "Your Majesty, there were three thousand, four hundred cases yesterday. This is getting to be alarming. Ought you not to return to Rome?" "You may go if you like," replied the king. "I shall remain till I see Naples free from cholera." And he kept his word.[35]

When a king descends his throne to serve those he rules and to risk his life, it is a grand picture of the meaning of humility. Isn't this what Jesus did for us? He stepped off his throne and humbled himself and became a man (see Philippians 2:6–8). In most kingdoms, the people offer their lives to save the king; King Jesus offered his life to save the people.

Humility has nothing to do with humiliation. It's *not* about maintaining a low self-esteem or having a lack of confidence. Jesus certainly did not suffer from low self-esteem, and yet he lived a life of complete humility. Many have come to view a humble Christian as a virtual doormat for others. In reality, a believer has a strong sense of self-worth and a secure position of identity as one who no longer feels the need to elevate the flesh or pump up personal pride. King Humbert was still the king, whether he was sitting on the throne in Rome or serving on his knees in the cholera ward in Naples. The state of his heart is what determined his true place and position.

With respect to our physical appearance, the word *modesty* connotes not flaunting our features, to avoid revealing ourselves in such a way that makes others uncomfortable or invites the wrong attention. Think of humility as the modesty of the heart. We work to not flaunt who we are, or be revealing of our self in a way to make others uncomfortable or to invite the wrong attention to who we are. For the Christian, humility means life is not "all about me," but rather all about God and others.

In Proverbs 15:33, Solomon sums it up this way: "Wisdom's instruction is to fear the LORD, and humility comes before honor."

KEY QUESTION: What does it mean to value others before myself?

Humility is the opposite of arrogance. An arrogant person wants their presence to dominate a room, while a humble person desires to make their contribution in a room to be about those who are in it. Practicing humility is not about blending into the wall and not being noticed; it's about being open and unassuming to bring out the best in those around us. Arrogance often makes assumptions as to what others may think or feel, while humility will make no such assumptions. A humble person is warm and welcoming to anyone with whom they come into contact.

When Jesus attended a dinner where people were jockeying for the best seats, he told a story about seeking the lowest place and then being invited to relocate to a better place. He summed up the teaching in these words: "For all those who exalt themselves will be humbled, and those who humble themselves will be exalted" (Luke 14:11). In Jesus' view, those who desire to exalt themselves are at the opposite extreme of those who are his followers. In the end, his kingdom will be revealed as contrary to the way things are in this present world. All those who have lived to be exalted will instead be humbled, while those who have served both him and neighbor will be rewarded.

KEY IDEA: I choose to esteem others above myself.

Scripture consistently connects humility and wisdom. Consider this insight of Solomon in Proverbs 11:2: "When pride comes, then comes disgrace, but with humility comes wisdom." Or this one from James in the New Testament: "Who is wise and understanding among you? Let them show it by their good life, by deeds done in the humility that comes from wisdom" (James 3:13). In a masterful way, wisdom brings together knowledge, life experience, and a personal skill set that allow a person to live life successfully. The wise person has a broad vision to be able to see their place and is not threatened by anyone else's position, for they are secure in their own. Thus, the wise person is free to be a humble person.

We would be hard-pressed to find anyone in Scripture more eligible for God's Hall of Fame than Moses. Even so, look at how Numbers 12:3 describes this pillar of the Old Testament: "Moses was a very humble man, more humble than anyone else on the face of the earth." This is a strong indicator of the fact that God chose him and blessed his life.

The man in Scripture who may have been the most humbled by God also ended up becoming one of the most effective men in the history of God's kingdom. When we are first introduced to Saul in Acts 7, he is overseeing Stephen's execution. This well-educated leader had taken on the mission to single-handedly wipe out all Christ followers. Acts 8:3 states, "Saul began to destroy the church. Going from house to house, he dragged off both men and women and put them in prison." But in Acts 9, everything changed. Humility came when Saul was confronted by Jesus.

> *"Who are you, Lord?" Saul asked.*
> *"I am Jesus, whom you are persecuting," he replied. "Now get up and go into the city, and you will be told what you must do."*
> *The men traveling with Saul stood there speechless; they heard the sound but did not see anyone. Saul got up from the ground, but when he opened his eyes he could see nothing. So they led him by the hand into Damascus. For three days he was blind, and did not eat or drink anything (Acts 9:1–9).*

Paul's teachable spirit brought him to the place to later write to the Romans, "By the grace given me I say to every one of you: Do not think of yourself more highly than you ought, but rather think of yourself with sober judgment, in accordance with the faith God has distributed to each of you" (Romans 12:3). What an amazing contrast, which once again proves the fruit that Christ can bring to a surrendered and submitted life!

KEY APPLICATION: What difference does this make in the way I live?

Humility brings a secure knowledge of identity in Christ.

Christ offers us a new life in all aspects, thus creating a new identity. His death and resurrection provide security now and into eternity. Our newfound knowledge of what he has done for us produces a grateful and humble state of the heart, as we continually find our life and breath in him, as Luke reminds us in the book of Acts: "In him we live and move and have our being" (Acts 17:28).

Humility brings the freedom to elevate and to esteem others.

With our new position in Christ, we now have all the resources we need to live out the greatest commandments — to love God and neighbor. The continual growth of humility allows us to feel no threat or insecurity in placing God's will and others' needs ahead of our own. We are set free in our souls to serve.

Humility redirects all our relationships to be about the well-being of others.

Once we learn to consistently esteem others above ourselves, the next step is to care for people in the way Jesus would have us care. We seek to serve all those with whom we are in relationship. We no longer use others as a means to our own end, but we make it a practice to ask how we can be a part of God's plan for people. We seek to follow Paul's advice: "No one should seek their own good, but the good of others" (1 Corinthians 10:24). We will see needs we never saw before, hear hurts we never heard before, speak life we never spoke before, and touch hearts in ways we never have before. This is simply modeling the life Christ led on earth.

Humility brings a deep sense of caring for the people in our circles.

As Jesus moved through the crowds, he had an amazing ability to find those with the greatest needs. From the woman who touched his garment, to Zacchaeus, to Nicodemus, to the woman caught living in adultery, no one was exempt from Jesus' attention and care. Income, education, gender, and cultural status had no bearing on his ministry to people. Everywhere he went, he looked out in compassion for those who needed him. This, too, is our job description, driven from a humble heart to serve as he served. From convenience store clerk to doctor, from homeless man or woman to politician, we treat everyone the same.

Humility brings a desire to reflect Christ in all things.

The ultimate humility is found when we place our heart in the constant position of putting God's glory first and seeking first his kingdom and his righteousness (see Matthew 6:33). The more we immerse ourselves into the ministry of Christ to others, the more we experience the abundant life he offers. Seeing him change lives through our obedience is humility at its finest hour.

For growing Christians, a strong sense of self-esteem flows from "God-esteem" on the inside, which frees us to focus on "others-esteem." When they enter any conversation with a neighbor, the prayer is, *Dear God, help me place this person above myself and draw them to you.* As the world becomes increasingly self-absorbed, humility will not only be one of the most attractive and refreshing virtues to a searching and hurting world, but also a great blessing to our own lives in offering our hearts daily to the Lord, as we exalt him and him alone. These verses of Scripture point us to this great blessing:

> Humility is the fear of the LORD;
>> its wages are riches and honor and life (Proverbs 22:4).
>
> All of you, clothe yourselves with humility toward one another, because,
>
>> "God opposes the proud
>>> but shows favor to the humble" (1 Peter 5:5).

Jesus humbled himself, and in due time, God the Father "exalted him to the highest place and gave him the name that is above every name" (Philippians 2:9). He promises to do the same for us: "Humble yourselves before the Lord, and he will lift you up" (James 4:10).

PART 4

Transformation

The Think, Act, Be Revolution

On this rock I will build my church, and the gates of Hades will not overcome it. I will give you the keys of the kingdom of heaven.

MATTHEW 16:18–19

The final two chapters will help us take all this teaching and strategize an application for our lives. The goal is to develop a plan for our own beliefs, practices, and virtues — to make the move from head to heart, for blessing others and glorifying God, as Jesus would have us do.

As we have now presented the virtues of Christ produced as fruit in our lives, let's begin with the completion of the Think, Act, Be Revolution.

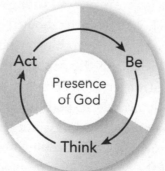

We now come to a complete rotation of change. Spiritual momentum and maturity begin to occur as the believer moves forward in the presence of God, while acting like Jesus brings a deepening sense of being like Jesus, driving the revolution on. Here we find the process of sanctification, where holiness and blessing forge an ever-strengthening foundation for the believer. This is the point where members of a community begin to see and agree that the virtues of God are indeed growing in quality and quantity on the branches of the believer. Heaven and earth agree you are being like Jesus.

Let's now zoom out and see how we, as these individual revolutions of change, fit into the big picture.

For our simplistic purposes here, let's define the church as "the collection of individual believers who are joined together in unity through their mutual faith in Jesus; the body of Christ, i.e., the extension of Christ's presence on earth commissioned to fulfill his purpose of living out and spreading the good news of salvation for all." In order for the church to look like Jesus to the world, individual believers in the church must commit to becoming more like Jesus in their own lives. The discipleship process to which Jesus commissioned his followers in Matthew 28:19–20 must have its full effect in the lives of each of the members. The Christian must progressively learn "to obey everything" Jesus has commanded to do.

While the old adage "we're only as strong as our weakest link" may not necessarily hold true throughout the global ministry of Christianity, there is still an overarching principle here: the stronger all individual believers are, the stronger the church at large is. To personalize, the stronger you become in Christ, the stronger you make the global church — the body of Christ. This worldview brings a greater level of accountability and purpose for your own personal spiritual growth. In short, you matter!

Peter was one of the first disciples to experience this individual revolution. Within a twenty-four-hour period, when Jesus needed his support the most, Peter publicly disowned him three times (see Matthew 26:69–75). An ordinary fisherman with high hopes of greatness, he was plagued with a common man's fear and insecurity. But after the promised Holy Spirit came on him in the upper room, Peter flung open the doors downstairs and powerfully proclaimed Jesus to a hostile world. The results were nothing short of miraculous. Peter grew daily, from being a rough, impetuous, impulsive fisherman with an ear-slicing temper to a faithful, steady, lover of people who spent the rest of his days standing for Jesus and who, in the end, laid down his life in his name.

The Presence of God

Peter tells us this same opportunity, this personal revolution he experienced, is available to all Christians — available to you.

> *His divine power has given us everything we need for a godly life through our knowledge of him who called us by his own glory and goodness. Through these he has given us his very great and precious promises, so that through them you may participate in the divine nature, having escaped the corruption in the world caused by evil desires (2 Peter 1:3–4).*

The same presence of God, alive in the middle of the camp of the ancient Israelites, is the same presence available to the individual follower of Jesus today. The same Holy Spirit to fall on Peter and empower him to live the Christian life is the same power alive in you and me. The resurrection life raising Jesus from the dead is in us! On our own, we don't have a prayer, but with the wind of the Holy Spirit at our backs, coupled with our committed and intentional effort, we can certainly make progress.

What is the reason or purpose for the powerful presence of God in our lives? Peter goes on to answer the question directly:

> *Make every effort to add to your faith goodness; and to goodness, knowledge; and to knowledge, self-control; and to self-control, perseverance; and to perseverance, godliness; and to godliness, mutual affection; and to mutual affection, love. For*

if you possess these qualities in increasing measure, they will keep you from being ineffective and unproductive in your knowledge of our Lord Jesus Christ (2 Peter 1:5–8).

The end objective of our spiritual growth is virtue — who we are becoming as people, which is, simply, "to be like Jesus." Paul stated the mission of the church this way: to be "in the pains of childbirth until Christ is formed in you" (Galatians 4:19). Jesus modeled these virtues perfectly during his time on earth; we merely seek to pattern our lives after him. The presence of God deposited in our lives at our conversion empowers and reveals this movement of change from the inside out.

Why is becoming like Jesus so important? Because his qualities are the ones that positively affect other people in our circles of influence and draw outsiders to want to belong to this community that consistently lives God's way. Qualities such as goodness, gentleness, and faithfulness may have little value in the world of a hermit, yet they are essential to the happiness of the people around us. Our spiritual growth is primarily for the sake of others and, thereby, glorifying to God. Ask yourself this simple question: "Am I happier when I hang out with impatient, arrogant, selfish, pessimistic people or with those filled with love, joy, gentleness, and peace?" Which people reflect the image of Christ? As each individual becomes more like Jesus, the place of belonging becomes contagious for those on the outside who long to belong.

It's appropriate here to insert a disclaimer to say Jesus warned us not everyone would be attracted to, or appreciative of, his life in us. There will always be those who despise anyone who is connected to Jesus (see Mark 13:13; Luke 6:22). Even as we realize this, we must not be swayed from our desire to both show him to and share him with a lost world.

The illustration on the next page displays the cycle of belonging, leading to growth, which moves us toward service — all of which results in a deepening sense of connection. In the process of moving toward growth is where we find the "Be" of "Think, Act, Be." And, of course, the nucleus, and the catalyst, of the entire process is the very presence of God.

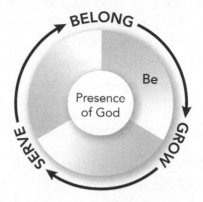

With this unique revolution — this ever-turning cycle of spiritual momentum — comes the opportunity for actual change. As we grow, we morph step-by-step into the likeness of Christ. This is a confirmation of our conversion and the evidence that the Holy Spirit is indeed within us. The kind of progress we make in this life matters to us, to those who are being influenced by us, and to those who have gone before us, whose legacy we follow.

Paul agrees with Peter's teachings and describes what happens when we are led by the Spirit instead of by the flesh:

> The acts of the flesh are obvious: sexual immorality, impurity and debauchery; idolatry and witchcraft; hatred, discord, jealousy, fits of rage, selfish ambition, dissensions, factions and envy; drunkenness, orgies, and the like. I warn you, as I did before, that those who live like this will not inherit the kingdom of God.
>
> But the fruit of the Spirit is love, joy, peace, forbearance, kindness, goodness, faithfulness, gentleness and self-control. Against such things there is no law. Those who belong to Christ Jesus have crucified the flesh with its passions and desires. Since we live by the Spirit, let us keep in step with the Spirit (Galatians 5:19–25).

Jesus completely and perfectly embodies the fruit of the Spirit. He possesses 100 percent of each one and displays each exactly as needed for any situation in life. Becoming like him in virtue, for the sake of the community — creating horizontal impact — and for the glory of God — bringing vertical intimacy — is the end objective of our pursuit of life in the Spirit. As this becomes a reality in our individual lives collectively, our community becomes the place to which we have always longed to belong.

The Revolution of the Mind

In his letter to the Philippians, Paul restates the goal of spiritual growth in these remarkable words:

> If you have any encouragement from being united with Christ, if any comfort from his love, if any common sharing in the Spirit, if any tenderness and compassion, then make my joy complete by being like-minded, having the same love, being one in spirit and of one mind. Do nothing out of selfish ambition or vain conceit. Rather, in humility value others above yourselves, not looking to your own interests but each of you to the interests of the others (Philippians 2:1 – 4).

He plainly tells us to value others and look to the interests of others. In the very next verse, he touts Jesus as the model: "In your relationships with one another, have the same mindset as Christ Jesus."

If we want to progressively *become* more like Jesus, we must progressively embrace the same *mind-set* as Jesus. If we want to *become* like Jesus, we must first *think* like Jesus.

Thus, in our illustration, we add "Think" to the process. This is not an intellectual pursuit, but rather, adopting the state of mind of Christ. As we belong, grow, and serve, we become, and then we start to think as Jesus would have us think. This leads us to serve others as we serve him.

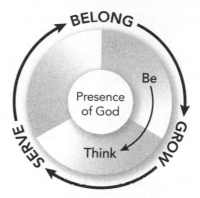

External virtue flows from an internal well of belief. If we *have* joy, for example, in our lives as seen by the people around us, it is because there is an internal belief acting as a nutrient flowing through us to produce this fruit in us. If we *lack* joy in our lives, as confirmed by the people around us, it is because there is an internal belief missing.

To use another example, let's consider a person who lacks the virtue of *humility*. This will likely be someone who lacks the belief in their new *identity in Christ*. Let me explain. When we become Christians through faith in Christ, we are taught that we become children of God and heirs of God's kingdom (see Romans 8:17). Therefore, we are significant because of our position as a child of God. People who lack humility often brag about their achievements and their associations with others. They often do this to gain significance. This lack of humility signals the absence of this particular Christian belief in the braggart's internal life. If the believer wants to grow in the virtue of humility, which is essential for healthy community, they will need to focus on the belief of identity in Christ.

The concepts Jesus and his apostles ask us to believe are the nutrients that produce the fruit of the Spirit in our lives for others to taste (see John 15:1 – 17). For every virtue God wants to see displayed on the outside of our lives, there must be at least one corresponding belief stirring within us. Inside produces outside. Fruit starts within the vine, unseen, before it emerges. If it isn't stirring within, the fruit will never mature and ripen on the branches of our lives for others to taste.

In the introduction, we presented the concept of a belief that begins in the head and travels to the heart to make a difference. Our mind initially takes in the information, processes it, seeks to understand it, and develops a point of view — thoughts and feelings about the proposition. The mind sends this information to the heart, which is the executive center of our will, for consideration of the idea. If the heart rejects the idea, we may say in public that we understand, or even believe it, but deep down, we don't. If our heart embraces the idea, then it will begin to form who we really are. It is automatic. We live from our heart. It's our default mode.

Remember the miser from the "Think Like Jesus" section in the introduction? He knows in his mind it is socially appropriate to be hospitable, which he knows is a virtue. He believes hospitality is the *right answer*, but he doesn't believe it as a *way of life*. In his heart he is a miser and eventually his true colors will emerge in his relationships with others. It's true for us as well; it's just how we are. We live only from the beliefs our hearts have embraced.

One day, as I returned home from a trip, I crossed paths at the airport with a man in the congregation where I serve. He mentioned to me my recent sermon about a somewhat controversial and countercultural issue. He complimented me by saying, "I've heard dozens of sermons on this topic and understood what was being said, but I never bought it." The man understood in his head each of the messages as "the right answer," but this time his heart embraced it. And because his heart has embraced it, application will become much easier. It will eventually become, as he grows in this truth, a way of life — a new default, if you will. This is why the wisdom writer pleads, "Above all else, guard your heart, for everything you do flows from it" (Proverbs 4:23).

Therefore, if you want to *be* like Jesus, you have to *think* like Jesus — from the heart. If you want to experience the fruit of the Spirit in your daily life, then you must believe in your heart what the Spirit also believes. If you want to be fit for life in the community God has formed in Christ, then you must exercise your heart muscle to pump the beliefs of God now. If you don't want to be a selfish miser who crushes the spirits of others, then you must guard your heart from the intrusion of the "acts of the flesh" (Galatians 5:19).

Again we see that what we truly believe begins in the mind, but it isn't an actual part of our lives until it makes the twelve-inch journey to set up residence in the heart. This occurs when a belief gets serious.

So the big question still remains: "How do we get a belief from our head to our heart?"

The Revolution of Actions

We *practice* our faith. When we observe the life of Jesus, we notice that he practiced a series of spiritual disciplines in his relationship with the Father and with other people. This illustration now contains the word "Act" to show our movement into service. The mind-set leads to action. And, again, all of this is brought about by and through the presence of God.

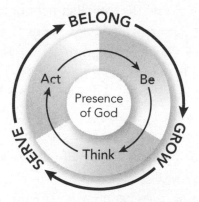

The practices Jesus modeled and taught, such as worship, prayer, Scripture memory, serving the needs of the poor, giving away time to help others in need, prioritizing our lives according to God's agenda, and even the act of total surrender, are offered to move the teachings of Jesus from the head to the heart. This is what it means to "obey everything" Jesus commanded (Matthew 28:19). If we want the nutrients of Christ to pump from our hearts to our hands, feet, mouths, and attitudes, we must remain in Jesus and keep his commands (see John 15:5, 9 – 10).

In the introduction, I shared the story of my own struggle with heaven and hope. Now, since we better understand the core belief of eternity, let's dig deeper here. Through faith in Christ, we are promised eternal life in God's new kingdom. This belief is a total game changer. If we truly believe this from the heart, it will produce in our lives the amazing virtue of hope. We can cope with the hardships of life and face the prospect of death because of the hope we have in Jesus Christ and the promise of eternal life. If we embrace this in our hearts, we can live with hope, even while facing the most difficult situations. Why? Because in the end, we win in Christ!

How do you move this belief of eternity from your head to your heart so you can truly experience hope? The answer: *Act like Jesus.* Read and meditate daily in God's Word about heaven, the return of Christ, and the establishment of the new kingdom. Soak in and sing out amazing songs about the promised life to come. Pray. Thank God for this promise, and invite him to show you more of what is to come. Get to know God better. The more you trust him, the more you will embrace and believe what he promised. Share your faith with a neighbor. Tell a friend about the hope within you and how you are growing in it. As you engage in these acts, little by little, the belief will anchor in your heart, where your life is lived.

Before you know it, someone will say in passing, "You know, you seem to be happier. Things don't seem to bother you like they used to. You seem to have more hope, and it's really encouraging to me. I'd love to spend more time with you." I hope is a fruit other people can see in you, and they can gain benefit from your example. You will notice it in your attitude and approach to life. You will have an extra bounce in your step.

So, in this example, you saw a lack of belief and fruit in the concept of eternity and hope. You decided to obey Jesus in this area. You took action. You read, memorized, prayed, sang, and shared. You applied. You grew. People were blessed.

We now see a complete rotation! The Think, Act, Be Revolution! We see in this experience the two meanings of the word *revolution* — first, the complete turning involved in the process of sanctification, as well as a radical life change of the soul. Do you see it? A revolution of a full cycle *and* a revolution of change are taking place.

Today, you have more hope than you did a year ago. You have become a little more like Christ, who faced each day, and even the cross, with an amazing sense of hope through the promise of his Father.

But this hope is not just for you alone. It is offered to the members of your family and to the community of believers to whom you belong. They find strength and encouragement in your newfound hope. But it doesn't stop there; people outside the church — your neighbors, fellow students, coworkers, extended family, folks who don't yet know Jesus — notice the difference and want what you have. You are becoming more like Jesus, which enhances the testimony of your life and the Christian community, so others see this and want to become a member of the family too.

Our goal is to *become* like Jesus. To *become* like Jesus, we must *act* like Jesus. To *act* like Jesus, from the heart, we must *think* like Jesus. We must practice the spiritual life consistently. As we do, these amazing truths, these beliefs, move from our head to our heart. When they arrive in our heart, out of which we live, real change begins to happen.

Empowered by the Spirit of God

Our own commitment alone is not enough to overcome temptations driven by our sin-filled, selfish hearts. This is where the presence of God comes in to empower the Think, Act, Be Revolution in our lives. God has established his presence within us, so we can overcome the power of our own flesh. Paul speaks powerfully about this in Romans 8:1 – 11:

> There is now no condemnation for those who are in Christ Jesus, because through Christ Jesus the law of the Spirit who gives life has set you free from the law of sin and death. For what the law was powerless to do because it was weakened by the flesh, God did by sending his own Son in the likeness of sinful flesh to be a sin offering. And so he condemned sin in the flesh, in order that the righteous requirement of the law might be fully met in us, who do not live according to the flesh but according to the Spirit.
>
> Those who live according to the flesh have their minds set on what the flesh desires; but those who live in accordance with the Spirit have their minds set on what the Spirit desires. The mind governed by the flesh is death, but the mind governed by the Spirit is life and peace. The mind governed by the flesh is hostile to God; it does not submit to God's law, nor can it do so. Those who are in the realm of the flesh cannot please God.
>
> You, however, are not in the realm of the flesh but are in the realm of the Spirit, if indeed the Spirit of God lives in you.

Without Christ, we are condemned and have no choice but to reside in the flesh. Our minds are bent toward selfish decisions. Our actions can only be of the flesh — the only spirit inside us. When Christ enters our lives, a new Spirit and a new way are introduced. We now have the choice to not live in bondage to the flesh but to resist it. We no longer live under the shroud of condemnation. Our minds can choose the Spirit. Our hearts can reflect the Spirit. Our actions can display the Spirit. Can we still choose to be ruled by the flesh? Certainly. But we now have the power and motivation to choose Christ — his mind, his heart, his actions.

Once again, we see the importance and centrality of the presence of God in the life of the believer.

The Revolution of Becoming

The Belong, Grow, Serve Revolution is a communal movement that comes straight out of Acts 2:42 – 47. The Christ followers in the early church devoted themselves to *belonging* — "to fellowship" and "to the breaking of bread." The same community of people devoted themselves to *growing* — "to the apostles' teaching" and "to prayer." Out of this context of belonging and growing, they began *serving* — meeting the needs of the people around them. These acts created favor among their neighbors. As a result, people were "added to their number daily," which brings us back to a deeper and more engaged desire to *belong* — thus producing a complete revolution.

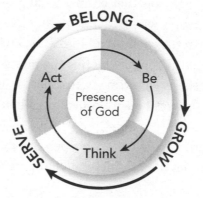

The Think, Act, Be Revolution is an individual movement inside the communal cycle. The wheel of the church spins by the force of individuals committing to become like Jesus. The new believer joins the church and thus *belongs*. This person then commits to *thinking* like Jesus in concert with the church (*grow*). They study the Scriptures and talk to God. That individual then engages in *acting* like Jesus, which not only results in *serving* others but now reinforces the beliefs into the heart from practice and experience.

The believer is now a bit more joyful, patient, kind, and so on, than a year before, enhancing the quality of belonging within the church family — and so we have the internal revolution of individual believers coupled with the external revolution of the church, driven by the very presence of God. The goal is for the cycle to happen repeatedly in the life of the believer over a lifetime. As the church collectively becomes more like Jesus, the outsider is more irresistibly drawn to want to belong.

God wants to get this Think, Act, Be Revolution turning in your life. He wants you to be more like Jesus — for your own sake, to be sure. He wants you to experience joy, peace, and hope daily. But he wants and needs you to be more like Jesus for the sake of others too — your mate, children, friends, neighbors, coworkers, and church members. The vision of belonging in the Christian community is special. It is not just a group of people who gather frequently or even get together simply to support a good cause; it is a gathering of people who treat each other like Jesus would treat others if he were in the room. And in reality, he is residing in you, so he *is* actually in the room, which is the point.

Would you rather spend time with a person who gives you the grace to make mistakes or with a person keeping score on every single move you make?

Would you rather hang out with a person who is filled with joy and optimistic about life or a person who is down on everything and negative?

God wants you to be a positive person for others! Such is his call on your life. Such is your mission, your central purpose.

For this to become a reality in our lives, we must install deep within our hearts the unique and truthful belief system taught in Scripture. We must *think* like Jesus. To move these key beliefs from our heads to our hearts, out of which we live, we must *act* like Jesus. We must practice the spiritual disciplines to convince our heart to go all-in for these truths. To buy in to them, not just understand them. And because the end objective of our spiritual growth is virtue, we must *be* like Jesus.

If we believe from the heart, we can make progress, as the passage from 2 Peter suggests early in this chapter. The human spirit is a powerful force. It can, on its own, build the Tower of Babel, but accomplishments like that will fall far short of God's grand vision for our lives (see Genesis 11:1 – 9). It is one thing to build a tower; it is another altogether to change a heart.

This is where the power of God's presence, dwelling in the center of our hearts, goes to work. As we yield our will — the same thing as our "heart" and "spirit" — to God's will, he takes control, just like the liquid spirits can do, as we discussed in our reflections on virtue 4 (self-control).

When an entire community of believers is unified and takes on this mind-set of Christ, not only is an ideal place created where we belong, but a revolution is also created, drawing others to long to belong as well.

The individual revolution of becoming creates the communal revolution of belonging within the church. Your personal Think, Act, Be Revolution begins when you "long" to "be" like Jesus, because you belong to Jesus. This truth and challenge set up our reflections in the final chapter.

Becoming a New Person in Christ

If anyone is in Christ, the new creation has come: The old has gone, the new is here!

2 CORINTHIANS 5:17

Jesus is inviting you to become a new person and to keep the Think, Act, Be Revolution turning until you go to be with him in eternity. He wants to:

- heal you from your *past* — to put pain, shame, and guilt in the rearview mirror

- make a difference in your *present* — to experience the fullness of Christ's blessing today

- invite you to be fully involved in his *future* plans — and to return to the garden in the new kingdom he is building for all eternity

Before Jesus left this earth, he gave his disciples an amazing promise and offered a compelling invitation:

"Do not let your hearts be troubled. You believe in God; believe also in me. My Father's house has many rooms; if that were not so, would I have told you that I am going there to prepare a place for you? And if I go and prepare a place for you, I will come back and take you to be with me that you also may be where I am. You know the way to the place where I am going" (John 14:1–4).

Jesus is not only preparing a place for you; he is also preparing *you* for that place. Little by little, day by day, through faith and the power of his presence, he wants to transform you into his image and likeness.

The entire movement of Jesus is empowered by his presence. Just as a giant wind turbine only turns as the unseen wind blows, so do our lives and the church turn from the wind of the moving of the Spirit. The wind of the Spirit is then activated in our lives when we do exactly what Jesus did every day of his life while on earth — submit his life to the will of the Father and rely on the power of the Holy Spirit to accomplish all things. Imagine millions of small "spiritual windmills" rotating in sync throughout every neighborhood in every city in the world. This is Christ's vision, and he is inviting you to take part in it.

I hope and pray that by this point in the book you are ready to declare your allegiance to Jesus and accept his invitation to begin the Think, Act, Be Revolution in your own life — to become a new person in Christ. He extends an invitation to you to truly live for a noble cause — the building of the kingdom of God. Jesus doesn't ask you to be a "dead offering" for his cause; he wants you to be a "living sacrifice" in his kingdom (Romans 12:1).

It's time to make a life-changing decision. You can't straddle the line. No riding the fence. Take out a pen — no pencils allowed — and circle your decision now. Choosing the bottom half signifies "I'm out," turning down Christ's invitation; choosing the top half signifies "I'm in," accepting his invitation in full.

If you circled "I'm out," the first question to answer is "Why?" Do you need more information? More time? Do you have some tough questions you need answered first? Concerned about having to give something up or start something new? I encourage you to look for a trusted Christian in your circles or a pastor or priest to get the answers you need. I invite you to continue seeking, but please know that Jesus' grace and mercy are available and ready for you at a moment's notice. I pray you find your answers and the Truth soon, so you can come to this line again and announce, "I'm in!"

If you circled "I'm in," make sure you tell someone right away. In fact, tell everybody! The apostle Paul writes, "It is with your heart that you believe and are justified, and it is with your mouth that you profess your faith and are saved" (Romans 10:10). For you, the next question may well be, "What now?" Deciding to change your life, as well as to join the mission to change the world, can be a bit overwhelming. Like a mosquito that flies into the middle of a nudist colony, you know what to do, but don't know where to start!

In this final chapter, I'd like to give you a few practical steps.

The V.I.M. Factor

I had the privilege several years ago to write the student version of the late Dallas Willard's amazing book titled *Renovation of the Heart*.[36] In the process of reading and rewriting this work of truth, I became convinced, once and for all, of the importance of the surrender of the *heart*, not just the *head*, in the Christian journey.

Dr. Willard lays out an important threefold process, using the word *vim*, to get believers motivated and moving. *Vim* comes from the Latin word *vis* and means "to have direction, strength, power, motivation, energy, and vigor." Willard cleverly uses the word as an acronym:

V — Vision
I — Intention
M — Means

Parents, teachers, and pastors often fail to move students along because we start with "the means" and ignore the vision. We give commands: make your bed, eat your vegetables, sit up straight, do your homework, read your Bible, do good deeds.

This strategy fails almost every time. It certainly did for me. I struggled in school. Frankly, I was bored out of my mind. Fortunately, with loving discipline, I made it through high school and eked into college. And an interesting thing happened there. I went to a university to become a pastor. By this time, I had a vision for my life. Suddenly, I had a clear picture of where I was going. All the classes made sense. I was motivated because I had an end goal in sight. After my two semesters of learning how to study, I earned straight A's and went on to get my master's degree — without anyone telling me I should or must.

Willard concludes that we often fail in our leadership because we put the means in front of the vision. Putting the "cart of means" before the "horse of vision" just doesn't work. Leading people by communicating the means alone is like pushing a string uphill — exasperating to student and teacher, child and parent.

We must begin with vision, and until we embrace this in the heart, transformation will be nearly impossible. So here we go.

V — Vision

The first step is to embrace the vision of Jesus for your life. Jesus wants you to *be* like him.

Ask yourself:

1. How would my life improve and my relationships be strengthened if I sacrificially and unconditionally loved and forgave others? (Love)

2. How would my life improve and my relationships be strengthened if I had inner contentment and purpose in spite of my circumstances? (Joy)

3. How would my life improve and my relationships be strengthened if I was free from anxiety, because things are right with God, others, and myself? (Peace)

4. How would my life improve and my relationships be strengthened if I took a long time to overheat and endured patiently under life's pressures? (Patience)

5. How would my life improve and my relationships be strengthened if I chose to do the right things in my relationships with others? (Kindness/Goodness)

6. How would my life improve and my relationships be strengthened if I established a good name with God and others, based on my long-term loyalty in those relationships? (Faithfulness)

7. How would my life improve and my relationships be strengthened if I was thoughtful, calm, and considerate in my dealings with others? (Gentleness)

8. How would my life improve and my relationships be strengthened if I had the power through Christ to control myself? (Self-Control)

9. How would my life improve and my relationships be strengthened if I coped with the hardships of life and faced with courage the prospect of death through the hope I have in Jesus Christ? (Hope)

10. How would my life improve and my relationships be strengthened if I chose to esteem others above myself? (Humility)

If you became this type of person, what difference would it make in your life? What difference would it make to the people around you? Then what if those folks also embraced this vision and offered the same virtues back to you? You would see a community filled with God's qualities. This is the description of life in the kingdom to come. Jesus is inviting you to start living this new way of life right now.

Do you truly want to be this as well? Is this your vision? Is becoming like Jesus more important to you than your career, how much money you make, how many degrees you collect? The list goes on. Have you grasped the implications, outcomes, and freedoms this vision offers you? Do you realize you will likely be more successful in every way if you become such a person?

For me as a parent, I can say without reservation that I want each of my children to be this kind of person. And for all who are not parents, I trust you can say that you want your loved ones to be like this as well. And if we want it for those we love, then we must show them the way by the pattern of our lives. The apostle Paul writes, "Join together in following my example, brothers and sisters, and just as you have us as a model, keep your eyes on those who live as we do" (Philippians 3:17).

On days when I'm willing to settle for less or take shortcuts to secure temporal outcomes, I remind myself of the legacy I'm passing to my children. It is good and right, but also biblical, to want to become like Jesus for the sake of others. Progressively, this vision is overtaking my life.

I love to golf — and even more so when I get to golf with my now adult children. The last time our two younger sons, who are both still single, were home, we went out golfing. Because we had one cart and three golfers, I chose to walk and invited my boys to ride in the cart. On hole five, the play coordinator met up with us. After talking to my sons, he approached me as I lagged behind with my bag on my back. He asked me why I was the one walking. Though I hesitated to tell him, in this instance I chose to reveal my heart and answered, "I want to model for them what it looks like for a man to serve his family." I must confess this is not the man I used to be. And yet now, I feel Christ is stirring in me to be more like him. And I not only want more, but I want *even* more for my children!

On the following page is a box representing your key vision, accompanied by a list of common options. You can only place one item from your heart into your vision box. What will it be?

- To be famous
- To be rich
- To make a difference
- To be like Jesus
- To succeed in my career
- To be smart
- To serve God
- To own a big house
- To drive the car of my dreams
- To be beautiful
- To be a celebrity
- To be a successful athlete
- To be married
- To have a family

While none of these are inherently wrong and most are absolutely good, the one vision Jesus says will properly drive them all is "to be like Jesus." Becoming like Jesus will bring a depth of satisfaction in our relationships with God and others. This sums up Scripture's goal for us. If you become like Jesus, all the other things will fall properly into place.

If you didn't select the "to be like Jesus" option, it's okay. Pretending will get you nowhere. In fact, many Christians say that Jesus is their vision, but daily live out one of the other options. Being honest is the first step to getting things right. It has to be the longing of *your* heart, not mine or anyone else's. You need to know, however, that unless you choose "to be like Jesus," the next two steps in this threefold process will be drudgery. If you did choose "to be like Jesus," the next letter in the VIM process will guide you into steady progress.

I—Intention

All four of our children developed a vision in their hearts for "independence" (i.e., getting their driver's license). They owned this vision, and so they intentionally made a point of getting their driver's license on the first day possible—the day of their sixteenth birthday. All of our children successfully achieved this goal —except our youngest. His sixteenth birthday was on a Sunday, and the DMV was closed—but he promptly got it on Monday morning. Yes, he was first in line!

Intention follows *Vision*. A person who has a vision but no intention is a mere dreamer. Our children needed more than just a vision for independence; they needed to form an intention and a plan. So it is with the spiritual life as well. We must be intentional—deliberate, premeditative, calculating, and purposeful— about becoming like Jesus. Peter sums it up this way:

> *Make every effort to add to your faith goodness; and to goodness, knowledge; and to knowledge, self-control; and to self-control, perseverance; and to perseverance, godliness; and to godliness, mutual affection; and to mutual affection, love. For if you possess these qualities in increasing measure, they will keep you from being ineffective and unproductive in your knowledge of our Lord Jesus Christ. But whoever does not have them is nearsighted and blind, forgetting that they have been cleansed from their past sins. Therefore, my brothers and sisters, make every effort to confirm your calling and election. For if you do these things, you will never stumble, and you will receive a rich welcome into the eternal kingdom of our Lord and Savior Jesus Christ (2 Peter 1:5–11).*

Rozanne, my wonderful bride of thirty-plus years, wanted to learn more about the specific areas in her life that needed attention and perhaps change. After completing a self-assessment tool, the results showed one fruit that was slightly bruised and in need of attention—the virtue of joy. Of the four statements defining biblical joy, my wife seemed to have the most difficulty with this one: "Circumstances do not dictate my mood."

In the assessment, Rozanne had received feedback from several close friends and family members. And frankly, we rated Rozanne lower on this statement than she had rated herself—which isn't an unusual thing to happen. For most of us, the area we need to grow in the most is the one we can't see—or at least can't see as clearly as others can. While we don't mean to, often we deceive ourselves. Self-introspection simply isn't sufficient to propel us to real and lasting change in our lives.

Rozanne went through a painful process in which she realized specific things in her life weren't aligning with the life of Jesus.

- Denial—"This is not true about me."

- Anger—"Who do you think you are, evaluating me so poorly?"

- Victimization—"Why are you picking on me?"

- Rationalization—"Yes, maybe it's true, but it's only because of circumstances I'm in."

- Acceptance—"The people who evaluated me took a risk and simply spoke the truth in love as they see my life. They care about me and only want to help. Oh my, this must be true about me!"

Eventually, Rozanne came to the place of acceptance, and I can still remember the day my wife owned up to this lack of joy in her life. She recognized that in Christ she had the power to overcome her circumstances and experience joy. And so she was able to move from *vision* ("to be like Jesus") to *intent* ("to have inner contentment and purpose in spite of circumstances").

Do you think people who intentionally establish a goal to move toward their vision are more likely to do better than those who don't? Regent University used the thirty key ideas highlighted in this book to conduct a study comparing those who had both a vision *and* a goal for their spiritual development with those who had only a vision but no particular plan for how they were going to grow. The findings? Those with a clear goal and intent grew considerably more than those who played it by ear.[37]

This was true for the early disciples, and it is true for Rozanne, for me, and for you as well. Vision must be followed up with laser-focused intention.

M—Means

To move beyond mere "good intentions," we need to put in place a thoughtful, practical plan for progressing toward Christlikeness. In Rozanne's struggle to experience joy, she came to accept the fact that she wasn't going to increase her level of joy by simply *trying* to be more joyful. There was an underlying belief that needed to be changed. The most common cause for a lack of joy is a weak belief in God as a good and a personal God. If a person truly believes in their heart that "God is involved in and cares about my daily life," it makes a huge difference in the level of joy they have. Rozanne knew she needed to identify the spiritual disciplines that could help move her belief of God as a personal God from her head to her heart. To do this, she needed to practice the skills of a joyful person. So she identified the means to move forward spiritually and experience the joy Christ promised. She identified four practices that especially helped her in this.

1. **Bible Study on a Personal God.** My teaching partner, Max Lucado, and I took our entire church through *The Story* experience in 2008 – 2009.[38] Through this experience, Rozanne discovered that all of her circumstances — negative and positive — were a part of God's Upper Story at work for her ultimate best inside her Lower Story. As she engaged in this study, she saw with renewed clarity how her attitude toward life's circumstances had robbed her of joy in the past, and she resolved to change her perspective.

2. **Bible Study on Joy.** Philippians is the Bible's treatise on joy. Ironically, the author, Paul, wrote this letter while he was under house arrest. Rozanne's Bible study focused on twenty practical disciplines for increasing a person's joy, and she not only learned about but also applied each one of them. In addition, she read a book titled *Truffles from Heaven*, which made her realize she was obsessing on her dark circumstances rather than on Christ and the blessings (truffles) he was sending her each day.[39] Carrying out this kind of mental discipline made all the difference for Rozanne, and it reflects the principle Paul teaches in Philippians 4:8 – 9:

> *Brothers and sisters, whatever is true, whatever is noble, whatever is right, whatever is pure, whatever is lovely, whatever is admirable—if anything is excellent or praiseworthy—think about such things. Whatever you have learned or received or heard from me, or seen in me—put it into practice. And the God of peace will be with you.*

3. **Worship and Prayer.** Rozanne engaged in a unique experience of worship that included a specific exercise program utilizing music to express who she is in Christ and his love for her. Through this discipline, she prayed and gave her daily burdens to him. And, of course, the endorphins released through exercise brought a more positive outlook on life.

4. **Biblical Community.** By confessing to her family and community both her struggle and desire to grow, she invited us to help her along the way. What I remember most was "the look." Whenever Rozanne began to let her circumstances get the best of her, the small group that knew of her goal to grow would simply raise their eyebrows (give her "the look") and say nothing.

My wife's intentional decision to grow in her experience of God's joy not only radically improved her own life but also the lives of those around her. I confess that I had seasons in the past when I'd look for an excuse to stay at the office a bit longer; today, I don't want to leave her side — ever. She is truly a "joy" to be with.

For all of us who are serious about becoming a new person in Christ, this process of sanctification doesn't happen overnight. Each step in this grace-filled walk will breathe life into our weary and guilt-ridden souls. I've found that I am still growing, even after many years of practicing this. Jesus is making me a better husband, father, friend, neighbor, and pastor as I learn to walk with him. Jesus doesn't dangle the Christian life in front of us like a carrot on a stick we can never capture. The abundant life is something that is available to us right now. Jesus offers it to you and to me today!

Yes! Come Quickly, Lord Jesus

What if a small band of folks around you joined you in this Think, Act, Be Revolution — a mutual rotation of belonging to Jesus and becoming like Jesus? What if a group in the neighborhood next to yours did so as well? And then the next. And the next. One revolution. Two revolutions. Three revolutions. Little by little, day by day, individuals and whole communities *thinking, acting,* and *being* more like Jesus.

Right now, the only decision you need to make is to say yes for yourself. If you are in — all-in — say it now, say it loud.

"Yes, I want to be like Jesus!"

"I want to think, act, and be — to become a new person in Christ!"

Acknowledgments

The average time frame for writing a book for me and most of my writing friends is around nine months. This book differs in that it represents a journey of more than twenty years. Many people have entered into my life, touched my life, and spoken into my life with their words, but mostly with their life lived out in front of me.

Rozanne and I met when I was only fifteen years old and only one year old spiritually. We have journeyed together every day since. Our mutual passion to become like Jesus is without question the number one marriage tip we would offer anyone. Rozanne has always been several steps ahead of me and has discipled me in many areas by her grace and her depth of love for me (the thought of which has just caused tears to well up in my eyes). I love you more today than when we met — not because you could be any more lovely, but because Christ has taught me how to love. I promise to keep my promise I made to you in 1981 to hold on to you till my last breath.

This book is dedicated to our four grown children — Jennifer, David, Stephen, and Austin. Rozanne and I were highly motivated to teach our children the amazing life offered in Christ. Our life together feels like a story line out of Deuteronomy 6: "Impress [these commandments] on your children. Talk about them when you sit at home and when you lie down and when you get up ..." Our prayer is for our children to pass these truths and life to their children — to our granddaughter, Ava, and to the one growing in the belly of our daughter, Jennifer — and to the twenty more to come (okay, that is a prayer request!).

To Desmond and Gretchen, the spouses of our two oldest children. We are so blessed to have you join us on our journey and us on yours.

To Mike and Bev Reilly. You have been such believers in and supporters of our family, I feel compelled to mention you every chance I get. The Frazee clan can never thank you enough for the deep love you have demonstrated to us over these last thirty years.

I must mention Bob Buford. He is responsible for inviting me into a think tank with some really smart people that got me to delegate the few brain cells I possess to this idea of people actually becoming like Jesus. Bob not only invited me in but also supported me and financed the adventure.

Some of the really smart people who spoke into my life and this framework are the late George Gallup Jr., the late Dallas Willard, J. I. Packer, Larry Crabb, and Greg Hawkins. You will see their fingerprints on the pages as you read. In God's wonderful plan, Greg and I, twenty years later, are working full-time on this, with the lofty hope of making some serious progress as God gives us lift.

To the staff of Pantego Bible Church. These folks were in the foxhole with me from the beginning when we were just shooting BBs at the target. Those were good days, and I will never forget your partnership in the gospel.

To the congregation of Oak Hills Church. God has brought us to you and you to us "for such a time as this." We continue to pursue the full implication of what it means to think, act, and be like Jesus not only in our individual lives but also as a community of believers. What if . . . ?

To my ministry partner and friend Max Lucado. Most people on the planet have read your amazing writings. I have the privilege of knowing the man behind the writings, and every day my mouth drops open in amazement as grace drips off your life.

To Mark Tidwell and the staff at Oak Hills Church. What this team does day in and day out is putting "legs" on the mission of this book in the everyday lives of real people. The best days are still ahead.

To Steve Green. You have walked with me step-by-step to bring these ideas and vision into a tangible work that people can use to help them grow. One of these days I'm going to write a simple book without forty supportive resources to accompany it. Not really — what fun would that be?

To my assistant, Nancy Zack. Nancy has flawlessly served alongside Rozanne and me for ten years. I don't even know what I am supposed to do or how I will get there after I finish writing these paragraphs. A quick call to Nancy will solve that. I think you get the picture.

To the man whose name appears on the cover of this book with me, Robert Noland. God collided our stories twenty years ago, and we became friends. We are just now discovering what God is up to with us. Your life embodies the words of this book. I couldn't have finished this on time without you.

To the team at Zondervan and HarperCollins Christian Publishing. The names are too numerous to mention individually. I should put the entire staff directory here because of the immense support I receive from so many departments. From CEO Mark Schoenwald to the person I have yet to meet, thank you. For this book in particular, I am deeply grateful for the keen insight of my editor, Ryan Pazdur, and to a wonderful man who is the final guy to touch everything I have ever done at Zondervan, Dirk Buursma.

Finally, to my God and Savior. I am so like Gideon of the Old Testament — one who is least qualified for this task, given my story. Yet my God loves to use the least likely folks to do his work. Thank you for letting me be a part of what you are up to. To you, God, be the glory!

— Randy Frazee

Deepest gratitude to my wife, Robin; my sons, Rhett and Rheed; Randy for his friendship, trust, and vision for discipleship; and Jesus, the one I long to think, act, and be like.

— Robert Noland

Taking It to the Next Level

Let me introduce you to a resource to use alongside this book as you turn your vision of faith into reality. Years ago, as these key ideas were formulating in my thinking, I was privileged to work alongside the late George Gallup Jr. to create an assessment tool to help Christians "make every effort" to become like Jesus. The end result was *The Christian Life Profile Assessment Tool Workbook*.[40]

The assessment tool gives opportunity to evaluate yourself in regard to the thirty key ideas presented in this book — beliefs, practices, and virtues. Each idea contains four biblically based statements. You do your assessment on a scale of 0 to 5. The higher the number, the stronger grasp you feel you have on a particular concept.

You then invite three people to assess you only on the ten virtues. Remember — virtues are the "fruit" of your life that others can see and "taste." No one else knows what you truly believe in your heart or if your spiritual practices are genuine, but they can tell whether or not you are gentle, joyful, or humble, for example.

You tally up and compare your responses with those of the three other people, and this creates your personal profile as compared to the profile of Jesus — the only person to whom you should compare yourself. As you see areas of strength confirmed, you will select one virtue on which to focus your attention. Your *intention* is to grow in this area, not to act out of condemnation or guilt, but rather out of vision and passion. The question is, "How much better might my life be, and others around me be, if I could grow to look more like Christ in this area?" You declare, "I can do all this through him who gives me strength" (Philippians 4:13).

Find a small group of like-minded folks and take the plunge. Engage with the *Christian Life Profile Assessment Tool Workbook* on your journey toward embracing your life in Christ — your quest to think, act, and be like Jesus.

Notes

1. Christianity Today graciously gave me three days of Dr. Packer's time when he was a "professor in residence" with them. His assignment was to give me feedback on the thirty key ideas described in this book and in *The Christian Life Profile Assessment Tool*, which I discuss in a bit more detail in the appendix. One of Dr. Packer's key insights was his suggestion that hope is a key virtue of the Christian life, which hadn't been on my list. As you read on, you will see the profound impact this feedback has had on my life.

2. I was deeply impacted by Dallas Willard's *The Spirit of the Disciplines*. Years ago, Willard was coming to Arlington, Texas, to give a speech. I paid the inviting group $500 to "purchase" some of Dr. Willard's time while he was in town. From the first meeting on, a wonderful relationship developed. Later I had the privilege of adapting Willard's outstanding book *Renovation of the Heart* into an interactive student edition.

3. This entire journey began years ago when I was challenged by a businessman named Bob Buford to find a way to measure spiritual growth. Bob led me to an outstanding book by George Gallup Jr. and Timothy Jones titled *The Saints Among Us*. Bob arranged for me to get together with Gallup on a number of occasions. Gallup formed my thinking on the transformation value of belief, practices, and virtues.

4. As I rewrote *Renovation of the Heart* for students, Dallas Willard taught me that "heart" is synonymous with "will" and "spirit" in the Scriptures.

5. Dallas Willard, *The Spirit of the Disciplines* (San Francisco: HarperSanFrancisco, 1990).

6. Greg L. Hawkins and Cally Parkinson, *Move: What 1,000 Churches Reveal about Spiritual Growth* (Grand Rapids: Zondervan, 2011), 19.

7. When a person attends seminary, they are exposed to a collection of classes under the title of Systematic Theology. These topics have been identified as central themes of Scripture. While there is no official list, here are the primary themes:
   1. Bibliology — the study of the Bible
   2. Theology Proper — the study of God
   3. Christology — the study of Christ

4. Pneumatology — the study of the Holy Spirit
5. Angelology — the study of angels
6. Anthropology — the study of humans
7. Harmartiology — the study of sin
8. Soteriology — the study of salvation
9. Ecclesiology — the study of the church
10. Eschatology — the study of end times

The key beliefs contained in this book draw from this list but focus more on personal transformation. We could call this list a "spiritual formation theology" instead of a systematic theology. That being said, I have combined some from the list above, eliminated two, and added a few subtopics that have great implications for our personal transformation in Christ. I worked for several years with a handful of spiritual giants to cull this list into the essential themes most affecting our spiritual transformation. Among these giants are J. I. Packer and Dallas Willard, who both endorsed these ten themes as the most essential, even though they approach things from different theological perspectives.

1. God — Theology Proper, Christology, and Pneumatology have been combined.
2. Personal God — One of the most unique and powerful themes under the study of God is his personal relationship with his creation. For practitioners of most other religions, their god is not seen as being personal and involved in their daily lives. So I've added this as a key belief.
3. Salvation — Harmartiology and Soteriology have been combined. The problem (sin) and the solution (salvation) have been brought together to form one seamless connection. Since this is more of a spiritual formation theology, I didn't want to single out the doctrine of sin as a primary category, which would suggest we need to develop in this area.
4. The Bible — same as Bibliology above
5. Identity in Christ — This is a powerful subtopic pulled out of Soteriology. The new person we become in Christ has major implications for our spiritual development; therefore, I've set it apart as its own topic.
6. Church — same as Ecclesiology above
7. Humanity — same as Anthropology above
8. Compassion — A dominant theme in both the Old and New Testaments is God's call on believers to reach out to the poor, oppressed, and needy. When this belief is embraced it creates a powerful reworking of how we spend our time.
9. Stewardship — This is another topic exported from the doctrine of salvation. Salvation speaks not just to our initial conversion (justification) but also to our whole journey (sanctification and ultimately glorification). When we express our faith in Christ, we acknowledge that everything about us now belongs to God. Obviously, this has powerful implications for the way we use our time and view our possessions.
10. Eternity — same as Eschatology above

8. In Roger E. Olson's helpful book *The Mosaic of Christian Belief* (Downers Grove, IL: InterVarsity, 2002), he sets out to identify the body of truth within these key themes of systematic theology that all Christians embrace or are unified around. Each chapter discusses what he believes to be acceptable diversity within these beliefs and what positions have been heretical or outside the scope of orthodox Christianity. Of course, there are some beliefs, such as the Trinity and the nature of Christ, that were highly debated by the early church in the first three centuries. I'm not saying that those Christians who took a divergent view were not Christians. However, the church ultimately landed on definitive positions within each of these areas. In this book I'm seeking to stay within the realm of beliefs that all, or at least most, Christians would embrace. On occasion, I confess to taking a bit of a deeper dive into a belief because I think it adds needed clarification and inspiration. When I do this, I'll try to be faithful and let the reader know.

9. A. W. Tozer, *The Knowledge of the Holy* (New York: HarperCollins, 1978), 1.

10. Frank Newport, "More Than 9 in 10 Americans Continue to Believe in God," June 3, 2011, www.gallup.com/poll/147887/americans-continue-believe-god. aspx (accessed May 5, 2014).

11. Stephen Seamands, in *Ministry in the Image of God* (Downers Grove, IL: InterVarsity, 2005), embraces this sociological view of the image of God in us and suggests we observe how the members of the Trinity relate to each other and adopt it as a model for how we relate to each other.

12. In this passage, Paul refers to the books of the Old Testament. Yet, as we study how Paul and the other apostles, like Peter, understood the writing of the New Testament in the same way, this passage certainly applies to the twenty-seven books of the New Testament as well (see 2 Peter 3:16).

13. F. F. Bruce, *The Books and the Parchments*, rev. ed. (Westwood, NJ: Revell, 1963).

14. Benjamin B. Warfield, *An Introduction to the Textual Criticism of the New Testament*, 7th ed. (London: Hodder & Stoughton, 1907), 12–13.

15. At the third council of Carthage in AD 397, agreement was reached on all twenty-seven New Testament books in our present-day Bible. Jerome's translation into Latin (AD 400) contained all sixty-six books.

16. Wycliffe, "The Worldwide Status of Bible Translation (2013)," www.wycliffe .org/About/Statistics.aspx (accessed May 8, 2014).

17. Søren Kierkegaard, *Provocations: Spiritual Writings of Kierkegaard*, ed. Charles E. Moore (Farmington, PA: Plough, 2002), 201.

18. Quoted in "3,600-Mile Ant Supercolony Found in Europe," April 15, 2002, *USA Today* online, http://usatoday30.usatoday.com/news/world/2002/04/15/ ant-colony.htm (accessed July 15, 2014).

19. Pew Research Center, "Millennials: Confident. Connected. Open to Change," www.pewsocialtrends.org/2010/02/24/millennials-confident-connected-open-to-change/ (accessed May 12, 2014).

20. Barbara Barton, *Pistol Packin' Preachers: Circuit Riders of Texas* (Lanham, MD: Taylor, 2005), 105–24.

21. Blaise Pascal, *Pénsees*, trans. W. F. Trotter (1670: repr., London: Dent, 1910), part III, §233.

22. Amazima Ministries, "Amazima Founder, Katie Davis," www.amazima.org/katiesstory.html (accessed May 14, 2014).

23. Carol Kelly-Gangi, *Mother Teresa: Her Essential Wisdom* (New York: Fall River, 2006), 2.

24. Frank Newport, "Mother Teresa Voted by American People as Most Admired Person of the Century," December 31, 1999, www.gallup.com/poll/3367/mother-teresa-voted-american-people-most-admired-person-century.aspx (accessed May 14, 2014).

25. Howard Dayton, quoted in *Leadership*, 2.2 (Spring 1981): 62; Francis Schaeffer Institute of Church Leadership, "Biblical Stewardship," http://biblicalstewardship.net/bible-passages-on-stewardship/ (accessed May 15, 2104).

26. There are a number of variations of this story, including one told in Henri Nouwen, *Clowning in Rome* (New York: Random House, 2000), 83–84.

27. Chris Carrier, "I Faced My Killer Again," Christianity Today International, April 22, 1997, www.christianity.com/11622274/ (accessed May 15, 2014).

28. Methodist Episcopal Church Missionary Society, *The Gospel in All Lands* (Charleston, SC: Nabu, 2012), 232.

29. The 700 Club, "Steve Saint: The Legacy of the Martyrs," www.cbn.com/700club/guests/bios/steve_saint010305.aspx (accessed May 15, 2014).

30. Dave Boehi, "Till Death Do Us Part," www.familylife.com/articles/topics/marriage/staying-married/commitment/till-death-do-us-part#.Utv_eXl6gUg (accessed May 15, 2014).

31. Urban Dictionary, "sticktoittiveness," www.urbandictionary.com/define.php ?term=sticktoittiveness (accessed May 15, 2014).

32. "The Spiritual State of the Union," a study conducted for The Center of Religion and Urban Civil Society at the University of Pennsylvania (Princeton, NJ: Gallup organization and the George H. Gallup International Institute, November 2002), 24, 29.

33. Larry Richards, *Expository Dictionary of Bible Words* (Grand Rapids: Zondervan, 1985), 303.

34. Ibid., 304.

35. John Stoddard, *John L. Stoddard's Lectures: Florence. Naples. Rome* (Boston: Balch Brothers, 1898), 149–50.

36. Dallas Willard, *Renovation of the Heart: Putting On the Character of Christ* (Colorado Springs: NavPress, 2002). Student edition: Dallas Willard and

Randy Frazee, *Renovation of the Heart: An Interactive Student Edition* (Colorado Springs: NavPress, 2005).

37. Richard L. Miller, *A Correlation Study to Examine the Relationship between Self-efficacy and Biblical Spiritual Development* (Virginia Beach: Regent University, 2003).

38. *The Story* is a thirty-one-week journey through the Bible; see Randy Frazee, *The Story Adult Curriculum Participant's Guide* (Grand Rapids: Zondervan, 2011).

39. Kali Schnieders, *Truffles from Heaven* (Enumclaw, WA: WinePress, 2007).

40. Randy Frazee, *The Christian Life Profile Assessment Tool Workbook* (Grand Rapids: Zondervan, 2005). An updated edition will be available in the summer of 2015.

BELIEVE

POWERED BY **Z** ZONDERVAN®

Dear Reader,

Notable researcher George Gallup Jr. summarized his findings on the state of American Christianity with this startling revelation: **"The stark fact is, many Christians don't know what they believe or why."**

The problem is not that people lack a hunger for God's Word. Research tells us that the number one thing people want from their church is for it to help them understand the Bible, and that Bible engagement is the number one catalyst for spiritual growth. Nothing else comes close.

This is why I am passionate about Believe—a Bible engagement experience to anchor every member of your family in the key teachings of the Bible.

Grounded in Scripture, Believe is a spiritual growth experience helping people of all ages become more like Jesus in their beliefs, actions, and character.

When these timeless truths are understood, believed in the heart, and applied to our daily living, they will transform a life, a family, a church, a city, a nation, and even our world.

Imagine thousands of churches and countless individuals all over the world finally able to declare—**"I know what I believe and why, and in God's strength I will seek to live it out all the days of my life."**

It could change the world.

In Him,

Randy Frazee
General Editor, Believe

LIVING THE STORY OF THE BIBLE TO BECOME LIKE JESUS

Teach your whole family how to think, act, and be like Jesus!

- **Adults** – Unlocks the 10 key beliefs, 10 key practices, and 10 key virtues of a Christian. Curriculum also available.
- **Think, Act, Be Like Jesus** – This companion to *Believe* helps readers develop a personal vision and a simple plan for getting started on their spiritual growth journey.
- **Students** – Contains the same Scriptures as the adult edition, but with transitions and fun features to engage students. Curriculum also available.
- **Children** – With a Kids' Edition for ages 8-12, a Storybook for ages 4-8, and three levels of curriculum, children of all ages will learn how to think, act, and be like Jesus.
- **Churches** – Believe is flexible, affordable, and easy to use with your church, in any ministry, from nursery to adults ... and even the whole church.
- **Spanish** – All Believe resources are also available in Spanish.

FOR ADULTS

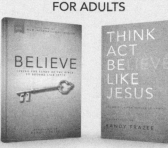

9780310433583   9780310250173

FOR STUDENTS

9780310745617
(Available May 2015)

FOR CHILDREN

9780310746010   9780310745907
(Available May 2015)   (Available May 2015)

FOR CHURCHES

Campaign Kit 9780310681717
(Available June 2015)

BelieveTheStory.com

BELIEVE
POWERED BY **ZONDERVAN**

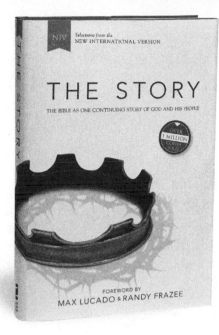

"THE GREATEST STORY EVER TOLD" IS MORE THAN JUST A CLICHÉ.

God goes to great lengths to rescue lost and hurting people. That is what *The Story* is all about—the story of the Bible, God's great love affair with humanity. Condensed into 31 accessible chapters, *The Story* sweeps you into the unfolding progression of Bible characters and events from Genesis to Revelation. Using the clear, accessible text of the NIV Bible, it allows the stories, poems, and teachings of the Bible to read like a novel. And like any good story, *The Story* is filled with intrigue, drama, conflict, romance, and redemption—and this story's true!

THE STORY

The Bible as One Continuing Story of God and His People

NIV Hardcover   9780310950974